THE PENINSULA CAMPAIGN

George Brinton McClellan, known as the "Young Napoleon" to his admirers and "Little Mac" to his troops.

GREAT CAMPAIGNS SERIES

The Atlanta Campaign
The Chancellorsville Campaign
Hitler's Blitzkrieg Campaigns
The Little Bighorn Campaign
The Philadelphia Campaign
The Peninsula Campaign
The Wilderness Campaign

GREAT CAMPAIGNS

THE PENINSULA CAMPAIGN

March – July 1862

David G. Martin

COMBINED
BOOKS

PUBLISHER'S NOTE

Combined Books, Inc., is dedicated to publishing books of distinction in history and military history. We are proud of the quality of writing and the quantity of information found in our books. Our books are manufactured with style and durability and are printed on acid-free paper. We like to think of our books as soldiers: not infantry grunts, but well dressed and well equipped avant garde. Our logo reflects our commitment to the modern and yet historic art of bookmaking.

We call ourselves Combined Books because we view the publishing enterprise as a "combined" effort of authors, publishers and readers. And we promise to bridge the gap between us–a gap which is all too seldom closed in contemporary publishing.

We would like to hear from our readers and invite you to write to us at our offices in Pennsylvania with your reactions, queries, comments, even complaints. All of your correspondence will be answered directly by a member of the Editorial Board or by the author.

Combined Books recognizes and appreciates the important and historical role of booksellers in the publishing enterprise. We encourage all of our readers to purchase our books from their local booksellers, and we hope that you let us know of booksellers in your area that might be interested in carrying our books. If you are unable to find a book in your area, please write to us.

For information, address:
COMBINED BOOKS, INC.
151 East 10th Avenue
Conshohocken, PA 19428

Copyright © 1992 by David G. Martin

Library of Congress Cataloging-in-Publication Data available.

ISBN 0-938289-09-8

First Edition   1   2   3   4   5

Printed in Hong Kong.

Campaign maps by Robert L. Pigeon, III

Contents

Maps

Preface to the Series

*J*onathan Swift termed war "that mad game the world so loves to play." He had a point. Universally condemned, it has nevertheless been almost as universally practiced. For good or ill, war has played a significant role in the shaping of history. Indeed, there is hardly a human institution which has not in some fashion been influenced and molded by war, even as it helped shape and mold war in turn. Yet the study of war has been as remarkably neglected as its practice commonplace. With a few outstanding exceptions, the history of wars and of military operations has until quite recently been largely the province of the inspired patriot or the regimental polemicist. Only in our times have serious, detailed, and objective accounts come to be considered the norm in the treatment of military history and related matters. Yet there still remains a gap in the literature, for there are two types of military history. One type is written from a very serious, highly technical, professional perspective and presupposes that the reader is deeply familiar with the background, technology and general situation. The other is perhaps less dry, but merely lightly reviews the events with the intention of informing and entertaining the layman. The qualitative gap between the two is vast. Moreover, there are professionals in both the military and academia whose credentials are limited to particular moments in the long, sad history of war, and there are laymen who have more than a passing understanding of the field; and then there is the concerned citizen,

5

interested in understanding the phenomenon in an age of unusual violence and unprecedented armaments. It is to bridge the gap between the two types of military history, and to reach the professional and the serious amateur and the concerned citizen alike, that this series, GREAT CAMPAIGNS, is designed. Each volume in the GREAT CAMPAIGNS series is thus not merely an account of a particular military operation, but a unique reference to the theory and practice of war in the period in question.

The GREAT CAMPAIGNS series is a distinctive contribution to the study of war and of military history, which will remain of value for many years to come.

Introduction

The Peninsula Campaign marks a watershed in the Civil War in several ways. After the battle of First Bull Run in July 1861 showed that the war would not end in a few short weeks, both sides raised large armies in the Virginia theater in preparation for the spring 1862 campaign. Union General George B. McClellan, commander of the *Army of the Potomac*, was determined to end the war in Napoleonic style with one massive drive on Richmond. In order to bypass the prepared Confederate defenses near Bull Run, McClellan in early March conducted the largest American amphibious operation before D-Day and transported over 100,000 men to Fort Monroe on the eastern tip of the Virginia peninsula bounded by the York and James Rivers. After he reached Richmond several weeks later he was faced by a Confederate force of over 90,000 men, the largest single army the South would field during the war.

The campaign featured a number of significant battles, few of which have received their due attention from historians. Though McClellan was a master of strategy, he allowed his army to be stalled in a protracted siege on the old Revolutionary War battlefield at Yorktown. The Confederates managed to withdraw before being overwhelmed and fought a successful rear guard action at Williamsburg; their stalling tactics at Yorktown had won the time needed to gather a defensive army before Richmond. McClellan then advanced slowly towards the Confederate capital until he was unexpectedly attacked by Confederate General Joe Johnston at

7

Seven Pines on the last day of May. The two day battle was technically a draw, but produced a most important result when Johnston was wounded and Robert E. Lee succeeded him as army commander.

Lee at once took control of the campaign and seized the initiative from McClellan just when the Federals had advanced to within sight of Richmond. Lee called Stonewall Jackson, fresh from his victories in the Shenandoah Valley, to the capital and at the end of June attacked McClellan's army and drove it back in the series of engagements known as the Seven Days' Battles—Mechanicsville, Gaines' Mill, Savage Station, Frayser's Farm, Malvern Hill. These were all important actions, some with more men involved than Shiloh or Gettysburg. In the end, Lee's plans to crush McClellan were frustrated, though he did manage to drive the Union army back from Richmond. The campaign showed that the war was not going to be brought to a swift conclusion. The conflict continued on for three more years, and it was not until 1864 that another Union army, led by U.S. Grant, would get as close to Richmond as McClellan did in the spring of 1862.

The Peninsula campaign should also be studied for its introduction of many elements of modern warfare. The duel between the *Monitor* and the *Merrimac*, fought at the very beginning of the campaign, was the first battle in history between ironclad warships. Artillery shells buried in the Confederate defenses at Yorktown were the first use of land mines in warfare. Both sides used observation balloons to monitor enemy movements, and the Confederates for the first time mounted a large cannon on a railroad car. All these innovations are discussed in the campaign narrative.

The campaign was in many ways a battle of psyches—pompous George McClellan, who mistakenly believed that he was constantly outnumbered, versus brilliant Robert E. Lee, who was unable to see his strategic plans carried out as he intended. Because it was fought in the war's second year, the campaign featured a large number of leading officers who are largely unfamiliar to Civil War students—Holmes, Huger, Magruder, G.W. Smith and Whiting on the Confederate side and Sumner, Heintzelman, Keyes, Porter and Franklin on the Union side. Yet there were also a number of more familiar players—Hunt, Kearny and Hooker in blue and Longstreet, A.P. Hill, D.H. Hill, Ewell and Stuart in gray; Stonewall Jackson's erratic performance in the campaign remains perplexing to this day. Above all, the campaign was fought by over 90,000 men on each side who formed the creme of America's young manhood, soldiers who had enlisted in their prime to defend their beliefs. Most were seeing their first action during the campaign, and in their innocent enthusiasm fought and bled in huge numbers—over 36,000 men fell during the Peninsula campaign, approximately one man out of every five engaged.

CHAPTER I

McClellan Takes Command

*T*he Civil War in Virginia did not go at all well for the Union armies in 1861. Brigadier General Irvin McDowell met defeat at the hands of the combined Confederate armies of Generals Joseph E. Johnston and P.G.T. Beauregard at Bull Run on 21 July, and his army went streaming back to Washington in alarming disarray. The Federals were fortunate that the Confederate army was as disorganized in victory as the Yankees were in defeat, and the incomplete defenses of Washington were not tested in the days following the battle. The Union forces desperately needed new leadership, and on 22 July Major General George B. McClellan, thirty-five-year-old victor in the recently completed Rich Mountain campaign in western Virginia, was hurriedly summoned to Washington to take charge of McDowell's disheartened command. McClellan proved to be an able administrator and reorganized the army well, but he could not be brought to begin a fall offensive against the Confederate troops that had advanced to the Potomac and the environs of Washington.

To be certain, McClellan's task of reorganizing what he christened the *"Army of the Potomac"* was not an easy one. He got along satisfactorily with President Lincoln, whom he had met before the war in Illinois but did not particularly care for because of his coarseness and lack of social graces. Much of McClellan's energy had to be spent trying to deal with crusty

A New Year's reception at the White House in 1862. Lincoln would spend most of the early New Year pressing for some substantial activity from the **Army of the Potomac.**

old Winfield Scott, who had been the commanding general of the United States army since 1841. Seventy-five-year-old Scott had developed the promising "Anaconda Plan", which called for a blockade of the Southern ports and the seizure of the Mississippi valley. Scott and McClellan disagreed strongly on the role of McClellan's army, as McClellan wanted to mass all the troops possible under his command for one Napoleonic style campaign that would capture the Confederate capital at Richmond and bring the war to a swift conclusion. Scott was also jealous of McClellan's energy and his meteoric rise to command, feelings that led to a number of quarrels that were soothed over only by President Lincoln's insistence. Their friction finally came to an end on 1 November, when Scott's resignation was accepted and McClellan was named his successor as head Union general.

McClellan's major shortcoming was that he was always reluctant to commit his army to battle. Due to faulty work by his chief intelligence officer, Allan Pinkerton (see sidebar at end of chapter), McClellan was firmly convinced that the Confederate army in northern Virginia was bigger than his, and he constantly called for reinforcements in men and equipment that were equally needed on other fronts. In reality, he outnumbered Johnston's army by an ever increasing difference, but he would never admit the fact. Lincoln at first accepted McClellan's arguments that he needed to reorganize the army before any advance could be considered. McClellan helped his chief engineer, Brigadier General John G. Barnard, lay out the defenses of Washington that would eventually embrace 33 miles of fortifications and emplacements for almost 500 guns. On 4 August he reorganized his command of about 60,000 men into 13 brigades. This number steadily increased by the substantial stream of regiments flowing into Washington, and on 15 October he reorganized his command into 10 field divisions.

McClellan took a firm hand to restore order and discipline in the motley array of volunteer regiments he inherited from McDowell. Weak and inefficient brigade and regimental officers were weeded out, and two crises dealing with the *2nd Maine* and *79th New York* "Highlanders" were successfully dealt with. The attention he paid to seeing that his soldiers were well officered, well trained, well equipped and well fed won him the respect, even the love, of most of his troops. He conducted frequent reviews to improve their morale, and the men were always pleased to see him gallop by on his black charger and tip his hat to acknowledge their cheers. To them he was "The Young Napoleon," and "Little Mac" was probably the most popular commander the *Army of the Potomac* ever had.

As summer turned into fall, President Lincoln and his advisors became increasingly insistent that McClellan put his large military machine into gear. He did not make any aggressive move until 30 September, when he occupied Munson's and Upton's Hills, two Confederate observation posts about five miles west of Arlington that had just been abandoned by the enemy. The army's advance encountered no Confederate opposition, yet it was met with widespread applause by a Northern populace that was eager for action. McClellan's

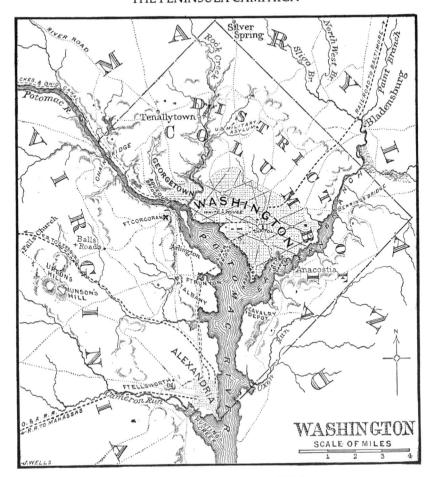

THE WASHINGTON AREA

"success" emboldened him to develop a plan to drive the enemy outposts from the Potomac River between Washington and Leesburg, and use that area as a base to move against the left flank of Johnston's Confederate army, most of which had withdrawn to lines at Centreville, just north of Manassas. His plans went awry, however, when Brigadier General Charles P. Stone mishandled a reconnaissance that resulted in the disaster at Ball's Bluff on 21 October, where President Lincoln's good friend Colonel Edward Baker was slain and hundreds of panicked Federal soldiers were killed when they were driven

Routed Federal troops flee into the Potomac after the battle of Ball's Bluff.

off the bluff and drowned in the Potomac.

The defeat at Ball's Bluff made McClellan reluctant to undertake further offensive operations that fall. During November most of his energy was spent in familiarizing himself with his new post as commander-in-chief of the army. In December he had to prepare himself to testify on the Ball's Bluff affair to the newly created but already influential Congressional Joint Committee on the Conduct of the War. He was scheduled to begin testifying on 23 December, but could not do so because he came down with a case of typhoid fever that kept him in bed for two weeks.

President Lincoln's impatience with McClellan's inactivity came to a head while the general was sick. The Northern press, led by Horace Greeley's New York *Tribune*, was clamoring for action. Secretary of the Treasury Salmon P. Chase gloomily predicted that the government would soon run out of money to pay for the war, and none of McClellan's senior officers seemed to know what their commander's plans were, if he indeed had any. At one cabinet meeting the distressed president exclaimed that if McClellan were not going to use his army, he would like to borrow it, "provided he could see how it would be made to do something." Lincoln even went so far as to canvass two of the army's senior commanders, Irvin McDowell and William B. Franklin, what they would do if they led the army. McDowell proposed a movement along the Occoquan River east of Manassas in order to get at Johnston's supply lines, a maneuver earlier proposed by the president, while Franklin favored a naval movement to the Virginia shore east of Richmond, a strategy briefly considered by McClellan a couple months earlier.

McClellan heard of Lincoln's meetings through his friend, Edwin Stanton (who would soon be named secretary of war to succeed Simon Cameron), and got out of his sick bed on 11 January 1862 in order to defend himself. His sudden appearance stunned both Lincoln and his advisors, who nevertheless pressed the general to divulge his plans. McClellan deftly managed to dodge their probes, and continued his inactivity. This angered Lincoln so much that on 27 January he issued a special Presidential War Order Number 1, which directed all Union armies to move forward on 22 February. Four days later, Lincoln issued his President's Special War Order Number 1, which ordered the *Army of the Potomac* to move on Manassas on or before 22 February. The president's intentions were clear, though the operational date did not take into consideration the poor weather and roads at that time of the year; it appears that Lincoln chose the date of 22 February solely for its patriotic significance as Washington's birthday!

If Lincoln planned to light a fire under McClellan with his two directives, he succeeded. On 31 January, the general submitted a 22 page proposal for an advance by sea to Urbanna, located on the lower Rappahannock River about 40 miles due east of Richmond. McClellan argued that a movement to bypass Johnston's large army at Manassas would save time, money, and lives; he correctly judged that "a battle gained at

Manassas will result merely in the possession of the field of combat—at best we can follow it up but slowly." On the other hand, his proposed coastal advance of 140,000 men to Urbanna offered the likelihood of ending the war in a decisive thirty-day campaign: "It is by no means certain that we can beat them at Manassas. On the other line I regard success as certain by all chances of war. We demoralize the enemy by forcing him to abandon his prepared position for one which we have chosen, in which all is in our favor, and where success must produce immediate results."

At this point, Lincoln was ready to support any strategy that would get McClellan moving, so he set aside his directives of 27 and 31 January. Lincoln's only reservation about McClellan's plan was that Washington had to be adequately guarded during the operation. McClellan promised to leave a sufficient force behind for the purpose, and spent the next month drawing up his final plans and arranging for sufficient naval transport to be gathered near Washington. On 8 March he presented his completed plans to a special war council convened at Fairfax Court House. The greatest objection to the plan was expressed by the army's head engineer, General Barnard, who correctly pointed out that Johnston would be able to use Virginia's railroad network to withdraw quickly from Manassas to Richmond, so negating the advantage gained by the proposed movement to Urbanna. McClellan's proposal to send a cavalry raid to cut the railroads did not convince Barnard, who joined Generals Sumner, Heintzelman and McDowell to vote against the Urbanna plan. They, however, were outvoted by eight officers who supported McClellan.

Lincoln met with McClellan's generals the next day and endorsed their decision, though he never was convinced that the Urbanna plan was superior to a move against Johnston's supply line via the lower Occoquan River. He acquiesced principally because the majority of the army's top generals approved the plan. He also was no doubt relieved to get

McClellan moving at last. As a follow up to the meeting, Lincoln issued two more presidential war orders. One directed that the *Army of the Potomac* should be formed into four corps, commanded by generals Irvin McDowell, Edwin Sumner, Samuel Heintzelman, and Erasmus Keyes; Nathaniel Banks would lead a fifth corps, comprised of the troops on the upper Potomac, and James Wadsworth would take command of the defenses of Washington. The other order directed "that no change of base of operations of the *Army of the Potomac* shall be made without leaving in and about Washington such a force as, in the opinion of the General-in-Chief and the commanders of the army corps, shall leave said city entirely secure." Furthermore, "No more than two army corps (about fifty thousand troops) of said *Army of the Potomac* shall be moved en route for a new base of operations until the navigation of the Potomac from Washington to the Chesapeake Bay shall be freed from the enemy's batteries and other obstructions." A final provision was that the operations "shall begin to move upon the bay as early as the 18th of March."

McClellan expressed great unhappiness at the president's orders. He had not been in a hurry to start the campaign, and he needed still more time to gather sufficient water transport. In addition, he would need at least two weeks to drive the Confederates back from the lower Potomac, and such an operation would run the risk of bringing on a general engagement with Johnston's army or possibly even of betraying the move to Urbanna. McClellan was also concerned that three of the new corps commanders, McDowell, Sumner and Heintzelman, had not shown any support for his Urbanna plan. Furthermore, he had not wanted to form corps until his divisions had seen combat and the generals had had a chance to exhibit their combat abilities. (It is interesting to note that Lee was restricted by Confederate law from creating corps in mid-1862, and did not do so until after the battle of Antietam.) McClellan was also annoyed because he did not much care for Wadsworth, an abolitionist who had no professional military training. He had promised the command of Washington's defenses to his friend Major General John A. Dix, but had not yet made the appointment official. This was one case where McClellan's well known procrastination finally caught up with him. Lincoln had simply run out of patience, and by his appointments deprived McClellan of the opportunity to secure corps commanders more favorable to himself and his plans.

The Numbers Game

Allan Pinkerton is remembered today as the founder of the Pinkerton Detective Agency. He was also a key figure during the early course of the Civil War, for it was Pinkerton who was mostly responsible for Union General George B. McClellan's exaggerated estimates of Confederate strength and his subsequent reluctance to take the field against a force he believed to be greater than his.

Pinkerton was born in Scotland in 1819. In 1843 political problems in Glasgow forced the newly married young man to emigrate to America. He settled in Illinois and became a successful cooper, but a religious controversy forced him to move and take up a job as a deputy sheriff. His abolitionist beliefs led him to become a key agent in the underground railroad, and his skills at sleuthing led him to open up a detective agency in Chicago in 1850. One of his specialties was to protect the U.S. mails, in this capacity he became well acquainted with George B. McClellan when the future general became vice president of the Illinois Central Railroad in 1857.

When the Civil War started, Pinkerton offered his services to the Federal government and was invited to come to Washington to organize the Secret Service. He met with President Lincoln and was promised support for his agency, but in all the confusion surrounding Fort Sumter and the se-cession crisis, no one carried through on the pledge. Pinkerton became annoyed, and instead of going to see the president about the problem, he headed back to Chicago. While on the way he received a request to come and see his old friend George B. McClellan, the newly appointed Federal commander in Ohio. McClellan offered him a post as the chief detective of the Department of Ohio, and Pinkerton accepted it.

Pinkerton came east with his mentor when McClellan was promoted to command the *Army of the Potomac* in the dark days following the Federal disaster at Bull Run on 21 July 1861. McClellan gave him the support he needed to set up the Secret Service, which Pinkerton organized in the provost marshall's office under cover of the alias "E.J. Allen." He hired agents and set up a successful espionage system that stretched from Baltimore to Richmond and beyond. He also specialized in counter espionage and was successful at catching the noted Confederate spy Rose Greenhow, who had been operating in Washington while relaying critical information to the Confederate army at Manassas.

Pinkerton gathered a wealth of military and economic information on the Confederate armies and regularly sent lengthy, detailed reports to McClellan. Much of the data was useful, but one important segment was grossly inaccurate and even misleading—the analysis of enemy strengths. Pinkerton's errors stemmed from two basic causes, the way he gathered information and the way he interpreted it. Much data was gathered from civilians, Confederate deserters, and runaway slaves, all of whom were given greater rewards for telling more detailed information. This encouraged the informants to exaggerate, and Pinkerton uncritically accepted their stories. Most of Pinkerton's agents in Richmond were not very creative or aggressive, and none had access to the precise figures McClellan needed. One agent swore that the Confederates had 160,000 troops in late August. Another, named Frank Ellis, insisted that the Confederate army had 80,000 men at Centreville on 28 October and 77,000 at the end of November. In reality Johnston's army was scarcely 45,000 during this period.

Pinkerton was inclined to accept these inflated Confederate strength figures because of methodological and arithmetic mistakes he was making at the time. He continually overestimated the number and size of the Confederate regiments, and then compounded his errors by adding five percent to the strength totals to make up for regiments he missed! On another report made in October he stated that he was reducing the Confederate strength total by 15 percent to account for their sick who could not bear arms, but he instead reduced the strength figure by one-fifteenth (6.7 percent). This one arithmetic mistake increased his Confederate strength figure by over eight percent.

McClellan accepted Pinkerton's inflated estimates at face value. To make matters worse, he decided to err on the side of caution and always preferred the higher figure when different sources presented varying enemy strength estimates at the same time. Thus when one operative gave an estimate of 123,000 Confederate troops in Virginia (a number actually only 10 percent high) and another agent reported their strength to be 180,000 to 200,000, McClellan chose to believe the higher figure.

McClellan added to his own problems by chronically understating the strength of his own army. When he had 192,000 men available at the end of December, he estimated that he had only about 100,000 on hand for field duty after deducting those on non-combat or detached duty (usually 10 percent), those not yet sufficiently equipped or drilled, and an additional 50,000 to 60,000 on garrison duty in Washington or elsewhere. He may have been deliberately underestimating his own field strength in order to pressure Lincoln into funneling more and more units into his army. McClellan wanted to have as many men as he could get before he joined battle with the enemy, no matter what the strength figure was that he reported to Lincoln and the War Department.

This unfortunate habit of overestimating enemy strength and underestimating his own played a key role in McClellan's inherent reluctance to commit his army to battle. By all reasonable accounts, he had about 100,000 men available to attack Johnston's 50,000 at Centreville in November and December. He nevertheless refused to consider an offensive that he probably would have won, because he firmly believed that Johnston had more men than were in his own command. McClellan at the same time was overestimating the number of cannons the Confederates had at Manassas, as well as the strength of their fortifications.

McClellan never did learn from his mistakes at estimating Confederates strengths in the fall of 1861. Throughout the Peninsula Campaign he moved slowly and deliberately because he was certain that he faced a superior Confederate force. That is why he prepared such an elaborate siege at Yorktown, even though he initially outnumbered Magruder's command at least 50,000 to 11,000. Interestingly, Lee's army actually did outnumber McClellan's army at the beginning of the Seven Days' Battles, after Jackson arrived from the Valley and before the Confederates began taking heavier losses than McClellan's army, but their lead was nowhere as great as McClellan believed. McClellan also gravely overestimated the Confederate strength at Antietam, where he believed that Lee had a stronger force than the Union army of 80,000, when in fact Lee had only about 45,000 men. As a result of this mistaken estimate, McClellan kept thousands of men in reserve during the war's bloodiest day of combat and declined to commit them to action when they could have carried the day for him.

Allan Pinkerton left the army in November 1862 when McClellan was relieved of command for the second and final time. He claimed in his memoirs that President Lincoln and Secretary of War Stanton urged him to stay on, but by then he was weary of the pressure of working under heavy responsibility on a limited budget. For much of the time he had been paying his own expenses and even the salaries of his agents from money out of his own pocket. He spent most of the rest of the war lobbying to get the government to pay what it owed him. He served as McClellan's chief of security during the latter's unsuccessful presidential campaign in 1864. Pinkerton was in New Orleans when he heard of President Lincoln's assassination in April 1865 and promptly offered his services to Secretary Stanton to help catch John Wilkes Booth. Stanton accepted his offer, but Pinkerton was too far away to help.

Allan Pinkerton, alias E.J. Allen, had a long and interesting post war career before he died in Chicago in 1884 at the age of 65. For more information on his life and the detective agency he founded, see *The Pinkertons: The Detective Dynasty That Made History*, by James D. Horan.

McClellan's Life before 1860

George B. McClellan was the most significant figure in the Union army in the East during the first two years of the Civil War. He was for a time general in chief of the Union army and commanded the *Army of the Potomac* for 17 months from July 1861 to November 1862. He may also have been the most popular commander that the *Army of the Potomac* had during the war. His career nevertheless remains clouded with controversy, and his strengths and faults are strenuously debated to this day.

George Brinton McClellan was born in Philadelphia on 3 December 1826, the son of a well to do physician. The McClellan ancestors had come from Scotland, and the general's more immediate forbears were residents of Connecticut. The most distinguished of the line was Samuel, George B.'s great-grandfather, who was a brigadier general of militia during the Revolutionary War. Samuel's sons, James and John, founded Woodstock Academy.

James' son George graduated from Yale in 1816 and then obtained a medical decree from the University of Pennsylvania. He set up office in Philadelphia, specializing in ophthalmology, and founded Jefferson Medical College. In 1820 he married Elizabeth Brinton, daughter of a leading Philadelphia family. The couple had five children (two daughters and three sons), of whom George

B. was the middle child.

George B. was educated at a series of prestigious private schools and entered the University of Pennsylvania in 1840 when he was only 13. He was resolved to become a lawyer, but two years later changed his mind and expressed a desire to attend West Point. His father approved, since the army offered a free education and the McClellan family fortune was beginning to wane under the strain of supporting five children. McClellan family connections helped George B. win his appointment, though he was only 15 years old at the time, several months under the academy's minimum entry age of 16. However, once he passed the school's physical and academic entrance exams, the entry age requirement was waived, and he entered the Class of 1846 at the age of 15 and one-half, the youngest member of the plebe class.

Classes at West Point posed no difficulty for McClellan because of the excellent schooling he had received in Philadelphia. He in fact thrived in his academics so much that he ranked third in his class after the first year, and graduated second. His upbringing also led him to enjoy the academy's social life as he gravitated towards the more wealthy of his classmates. He tended for some reason to prefer Southerners over Northerners; his closest friends included Ambrose Powell Hill of Virginia and

Cadmus Wilcox of North Carolina, both of whom would become foes fifteen years later. In fact, of the 59 graduates of McClellan's class of 1846, no less than 20 would become generals in the Civil War. These included Jesse Reno, Darius Couch, and George Stoneman on the Union side, and David R. Jones and Thomas J. Jackson on the Confederate side, not to omit George Pickett, who graduated at the bottom of the class.

Upon graduation, McClellan was commissioned a second lieutenant of Engineers, but was at once set to work drilling militia volunteers for the newly declared war with Mexico. In September 1846 he was finally sent to Texas, only to fall victim to dysentery and malaria, the latter of which would trouble him for the rest of his left. In the spring of 1847 he was well enough to join Winfield Scott's siege of Veracruz, where he worked under the supervision of Captain Robert E. Lee. He served well during the ensuing drive on Mexico City, being slightly wounded at Contreras on 19 August, and earned the rank of Brevet Captain for his courage at Chapultepec. The greatest lessons he learned from the campaign were a dislike of militia generals and a preference for sieges over frontal assaults. Both principles would affect his thinking as army commander during the Civil War.

Army life after the challenges of the Mexican War proved to be somewhat dull for Captain McClellan. He desired to be posted someplace where there was at least

some activity, but he was ordered to report to West Point as a junior instructor in engineering and mathematics. The appointment was an honor, though he chafed at the haughtiness of the senior professors. He did manage to form a firm friendship with two fellow junior instructors, William Franklin and Fitz-John Porter, both of whom were destined to become corps commanders during the Peninsular Campaign. He used much of his free time to study military history, and also translated into English a French manual on bayonet exercises.

In 1851 McClellan was transferred to Fort Delaware, an uncompleted masonry fort near Wilmington. The post offered him the opportunity to do a lot of hunting and to take up the study of German. A year later he was reassigned to Fort Smith, Arkansas, to take part in an expedition to locate the sources of the Red River. When that job was finished, he conducted a survey of the coast of Texas. In 1853 he was ordered to direct a survey of a railroad route through Washington State; his quartermaster during this expedition was Ulysses S. Grant, who once got so drunk that the offended McClellan never forgave him. The survey was not particularly successful because of McClellan's reluctance to enter and explore the mountain wilderness.

After a surveying project in the Dominican Republic in 1854, McClellan decided that he was weary of engineering and requested a transfer to another branch of the service. He got his wish the next year through the help of his new mentor, Secretary of War Jefferson Davis, who secured for him an appointment as a captain in the *1st U.S. Cavalry*. The next year Davis did him still another favor by appointing him to a three man commission being sent to observe the Crimean War. McClellan learned much from the experience, and was particularly interested in the extensive siege works at Sevastopol. He returned to the United States in 1856 after a grand tour of European capitals, and set to work on a lengthy report on the organization of Europe's principal armies, a project that was published as a congressional document. One of his recommendations in the section on cavalry was the adoption of a special saddle adapted from Hungarian and Prussian forms. This "McClellan saddle" was adopted by the military and was used for a number of years by the cavalry—a curious outcome considering the fact that its inventor never served a day in the field with his unit, the *1st U.S. Cavalry*. Upon the completion of his European report, McClellan resigned from the army in January 1857 to seek more lucrative civilian employment.

McClellan pondered a number of job prospects in the civilian world, and decided to accept a position as chief engineer for the Illinois Central Railroad, a post he came across through the recommendation of friends from his Mexican War days. His pay was $3,000 a year, twice his army sal-

ary, with prospects for promotion and more pay increases. He moved to Chicago in early 1857, and proved to be so energetic and capable that he was soon named a vice president of the railroad. His company barely weathered the Panic of 1857, after which McClellan aggressively expanded its connections and services. He at times grew restless with civilian life and looked to obtain various army commissions, but none of his plans worked out, so he stayed with the railroad, placated by the good pay.

In 1858 McClellan hired an old army friend, Ambrose E. Burnside, whose gun manufacturing company had gone bankrupt the year before. He offered to share his large Chicago home with Burnside until the latter got settled, and the two became even closer. During this period McClellan worked with two other Illinoisans with whom he would have significant contact later—detective Allan Pinkerton, who was in charge of security for the railroad, and a Springfield lawyer named Abraham Lincoln, who represented the Illinois Central in several lawsuits. McClellan later wrote of his early acquaintance with the future president: "More than once I have been with him in out-of-the-way county seats where some important case was being tried, and, in the lack of sleeping accommodations, have spent the night in front of a stove listening to the unceasing flow of anecdotes from his lips...His stories were seldom refined but were always to the point." It is understandable that McClellan was not much impressed with Lincoln's lack of refinement, an attitude he maintained even after he was appointed the army's head general, when he would often refer to the president as a "barbarian" or a "gorilla." On one occasion he even came home from a party and went straight to bed even though he knew that Lincoln was in the parlor waiting to see him!

McClellan was now ready to marry, and he turned his attention to the attractive Ellen Marcy, daughter of one of his older army comrades. He had been a friend of the Marcy's for years, and had been courting Ellen off and on for some time. Ellen, however, was not enamored of him, and in 1856 became engaged to McClellan's good friend A.P. Hill. When Ellen was forced to break off her engagement after she learned that Hill had a venereal disease, McClellan renewed his efforts with the support of her parents. She finally gave in to his persistence three years later, and the couple were married in New York in May of 1860. Their wedding guests included General Winfield Scott and future Confederate generals D.H. Hill and Joe Johnston. Despite their long courtship, George and Ellen were very devoted to each other, and wrote each other daily when they were apart. The couple had two children, a daughter, Mary (called May), born in 1861, and a son, George B. Jr. (called Max), born in 1865.

Soon after he was married, McClellan resigned his position with the Illinois Central Railroad to become superintendent of the Ohio and Mississippi Railroad at a salary of $10,000 a year, twice his previous wage. In August 1860 he moved with his wife to Cincinnati, where they lived a happy life until the war broke out.

CHAPTER II

All Quiet on the Potomac

The Confederate army in northern Virginia was neither as strong nor as well equipped as Union General George B. McClellan thought. In late July, the Confederate forces near Manassas numbered only about 40,000 men, whereas McClellan believed they had 100,000 and 100 cannons. The Confederate commander, General Joseph E. Johnston, was hampered by a severe lack of supplies caused by an inefficient commissary general, L.B. Northrop, in Richmond. Johnston later wrote that up until 10 August—almost three weeks after the Confederate victory at Bull Run—the army seldom had as much as two days' rations, and did not possess half the ammunition necessary for a battle.

This lack of supplies, combined with a healthy respect for the growing strength of the Union fortifications at Washington, caused Johnston to be hesitant to move his men north from their camps near Manassas until mid-August. At length, he was encouraged by McClellan's lack of aggressiveness, and moved his base camp from Manassas to Centreville. At the beginning of September he advanced several brigades to Fairfax, eight miles east of Centreville, and pushed James Longstreet's brigade and Jeb Stuart's 1st Virginia Cavalry to Fall's Church. Longstreet's advanced outposts were stationed at Munson's Hill, just five miles from the Long Bridge across the Potomac at Washington. His pickets were within sight of the Federal capital, a fact that gave a great sense of jubilation to the entire Confederate army.

An embarrassment to the Union, the Confederate fort at Munson's Hill was only five miles from Washington, D.C.

Johnston's advance threw Washington into an uproar. Many congressmen and newspapers considered it to be a national disgrace to allow the enemy to be so close to the national capital. General McClellan, however, was not inclined to take immediate measures to drive the Confederates back. He was certain that the Southerners would not have made such a bold move unless they possessed a strong army. The situation, in fact, gave him the opportunity to demand—and receive—the heavy reinforcements of men and material that he earnestly desired.

The fact of the matter was that McClellan could have brushed back the Confederate outposts at any time. Johnston was well aware of this fact, and ordered Longstreet not to attempt an advance on Alexandria or provoke the enemy in any way. The purpose of his outposts was solely to embarrass the enemy and to prevent the Yankees from making any surprise attacks on the main Confederate army. Longstreet and Stuart carried out their mission well. Stuart set up an aggressive picket line and won a minor victory at Lewinsville on 11 September by driving back a Union reconnaissance. Longstreet, who had only one battery of artillery with him, improvised some "dummy" batteries that successfully fooled the enemy: "We collected a number of wagon-wheels and mounted on them stove-pipes of different calibre to threaten Alexandria, and even the National capital and Executive Mansion. It is needless to say that Munson's Hill was so safe as not to disturb our profound slumbers."

McClellan's passiveness in September convinced even Johnston that an offensive might be successfully launched. As a prelude to more active operations, he divided his 13 brigades into 4 divisions, commanded by Major Generals Earl Van Dorn, G. W. Smith, James Longstreet and Thomas J. "Stonewall" Jackson. Johnston's plan, originally advocated by his second-in-command, General P.G.T. Beauregard, was to cross the Potomac above Washington, enter Maryland, and threaten the Federal capital from its less fortified northwestern approaches. The plan was formulated in late September, and on 1 October the two generals met with President Jefferson Davis at Fairfax to present their strategy. Davis agreed that it would be to the South's advantage to conduct an offensive before the winter set in, but he balked at stripping the nation's other armies to provide the additional 20,000 men Johnston and Beauregard said they needed in order to conduct the campaign.

Johnston at once understood that Davis' refusal to provide reinforcements meant more than the scrapping of his plans for an offensive. Growing Federal strength was making it increasingly hazardous to continue to hold his advanced position facing Washington. On 20 September he had found it necessary to withdraw his outpost at Munson's Hill, and he also pulled Longstreet's command back to Fairfax. This move delighted the Yankees, who promptly conducted a "glorious advance" to occupy the deserted Confederate positions. The Southerners remained on the alert, and particularly annoyed the Yankees by blocking traffic on the Potomac with river batteries and a strong force stationed at Leesburg, above the capital.

Joseph E. Johnston

Joseph Eggleston Johnston, commander of the leading Confederate army in Virginia from First Bull Run to Seven Pines, was born near Farmville, Virginia, on 3 February 1807, and was just 15 days younger than Robert E. Lee. He attended West Point in the same class as Lee, and graduated 13th in the Class of 1829 (Lee was second). His extensive pre-Civil War military career included service in the Black Hawk War, the Seminole War, and very active campaigning in the Mexican War, where he was wounded five times and led an assaulting column at Chapultepec. Following the war, he became one of the army's senior officers, serving as chief of topographical engineers in Texas and then as lieutenant colonel of the 1st U.S. Cavalry. When the Civil War broke out, he was a newly appointed brigadier general and the quartermaster general of the United States Army.

Johnston resigned from the U.S. Army in the days following Fort Sumter and accepted a commission as a Brigadier General in the Confederate army. He was assigned to command a small army in the Shenandoah Valley, where he was watched by a Union army under Robert Patterson. He managed to slip away from Patterson and join Beauregard's army at Manassas just in time to help defeat McDowell at First Bull Run on 21 July 1861. Johnston was overall commander on the field that day, and the victory would be his greatest triumph of the war. The victory won him a promotion to full general on 31 August, and he ranked fourth in the Confederate service behind Adjutant General Samuel Cooper, Albert S. Johnston (no relation), and Robert E. Lee. Joe Johnston, however, objected to his subordinate status; he bitterly claimed that his rank in the prewar army was senior to those placed over him and that he should have received the highest position. His protestations set off a running quarrel with President Jefferson Davis that would last the entire war.

Johnston remained in command of Virginia's largest field army until he was wounded at the battle of Seven Pines on 31 May 1862. His bad luck was Robert E. Lee's good fortune, as Lee took over com-

30

By mid-October, Johnston decided that it was becoming too dangerous to hold his advanced position at Fairfax any longer in the face of a largely superior enemy force. He had previously directed his engineers to prepare defensive lines at Centreville, and on 19 October he withdrew the forces at

mand of Johnston's army and would lead it to the end of the war.

When he recovered from his wound that fall, Johnston was assigned to be commander of the Confederacy's Department of the West, where he had the unenviable job of trying to coordinate Braxton Bragg's army in Tennessee and John Pemberton's in Mississippi. The South simply lacked the resources to hold back U.S. Grant and his generals in the west, and Johnston's subordinates lost battle after battle at Stones River, Vicksburg and Chattanooga; their only victory was Bragg's at Chickamauga in the fall of 1863. During this period Johnston led a field army only once, during an unsuccessful attempt to relieve Pemberton during the siege of Vicksburg.

In late 1863 Johnston was directed to take charge of the Army of Tennessee and try to defend Atlanta. He fought a skillful defensive campaign against Sherman in the spring of 1864, but his style did not suit President Davis, and he was unable to keep the loyalty of his diverse generals, who continually quarreled with him and with each other. He was replaced as army commander in July 1864 by John B. Hood, who proceeded to destroy the army in futile as-

saults against the Federals at Atlanta, Franklin and Nashville. Johnston nevertheless remained loyal to his country, and buried his pride to accept command of the Army of Tennessee during the last three months of the war. He surrendered to Sherman at Bentonville, North Carolina, on 26 April 1865.

Following the war, Johnston lived a varied and rewarding life as an insurance salesman, U.S. Congressman from Virginia, and railroad commissioner. He spent a great deal of effort at defending his military career in his autobiography (published in 1874) and several long articles in the popular series *Battles and Leaders of the Civil War*. He died in 1891 from pneumonia he contracted while standing hatless at the funeral of his onetime foe, William T. Sherman. He is buried in Baltimore.

Johnston was a capable administrator who may have been promoted beyond his abilities to high army and departmental command. He was not aggressive enough by nature to take the risks necessary to win great victories, and he was so high strung that he could not work easily with President Davis, Braxton Bragg, and other rivals who had a similar temperament.

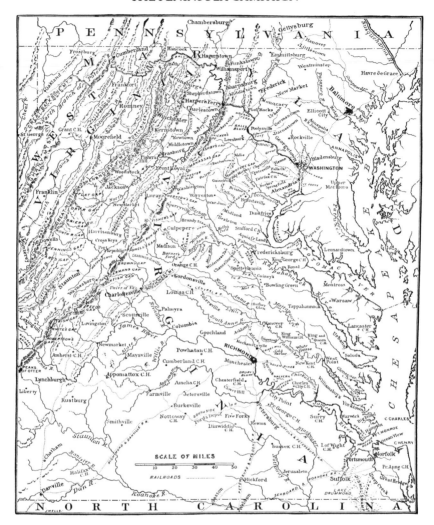

THE CAMPAIGN IN VIRGINIA

Fairfax to the new position. The move was made so carefully that McClellan at first was not aware of it. The Union commander at the time was preoccupied with an operation designed to drive the Confederates out of Leesburg, located south of the Potomac to the west of Washington. The Union maneuver began on the 19th when McClellan sent McCall's division to Dranesville; the next day he ordered Stone's division, stationed north of the Potomac opposite Leesburg, to make a reconnaissance across the river in support of McCall. McCall might have given "Shanks" Evans, the Confederate commander at Leesburg, a rough time if he had advanced beyond Dranesville. Instead, McClellan grew wary that Mc-Call might be cut off by the main Confederate army, so he withdrew McCall on the 20th. His failure to inform Stone of McCall's withdrawal led to the Union disaster at Ball's Bluff, mentioned in chapter I.

Johnston was confident of the strength of his position at Centreville, and actually hoped that McClellan would come forward to attack him. He had fortifications built on the crest of the hill near the village, and placed three of his divisions in the front line—Van Dorn and Longstreet held the ground on the right from Union mills to Centreville, and Smith held the line to the left of the village; Jackson was in reserve. Johnston did not possess enough artillery to cover the entire line, so he prepared a number of dummy wooden guns (called "Quaker" guns), just as Longstreet had done at Munson's Hill. The ruse worked, and McClellan was convinced that the Confederates had over 200 guns in their works at Centreville. McClellan also thought that Johnston had at least 100,000 men there, whereas Johnston actually fielded only about 37,000 (not including 6,000 on the lower Occoquan and 3,000 at Leesburg). Any aggressiveness McClellan possessed was chastened by the debacle at Ball's Bluff, and the Yankees would make no hostile moves in the theater for the next four months despite their overwhelming superiority in men and cannons.

As soon as his army was settled at Centreville, Johnston set about reorganizing it, a task he had been reluctant to carry out while he had troops in front of Washington. On 22 October he obtained permission from the War Department to extend his command, which would be designated the "Department of Northern Virginia." The department would consist of three subdistricts: Brigadier General Theophilus Holmes' force of 6,000 stationed near Fredericksburg, Major

General "Stonewall" Jackson's Valley District, and the central "Potomac District," which would embrace the principal army at Centreville. General P.G.T. Beauregard was assigned to command the Potomac District, but he was not pleased with the post because he had previously been serving as Johnston's second-in-command and viewed the new job as a demotion. In addition, Johnston made his headquarters at Centreville and gave orders directly to the army, thus making Beauregard's office superfluous. Beauregard's subsequent complaints to Richmond embroiled much of the Confederate congress and began agitating President Davis. At length, the awkward situation was resolved in January 1862 when Davis transferred Beauregard to Tennessee, where he would serve as Albert S. Johnston's second-in-command during the Shiloh campaign.

Johnston spent the rest of October and all of November 1861 expanding and strengthening his position near Centreville. His lines would eventually extend almost 25 miles and would give his troops (many of whom were newly raised or had not seen action at Bull Run) a great deal of confidence. Johnston also continued to support his outposts at Leesburg and along the lower Potomac, which succeeded in closing the river to enemy commercial traffic and were causing "a deep feeling of mortification and humiliation" in Washington. Several Northern newspapers criticized McClellan's failure to take action by continually running the headline "All Quiet on the Potomac" in their reports of war news.

The weather was suitable for operations until well into December. Since he had been refused the reinforcements he needed in order to take the offensive, Johnston was compelled to wait at Centreville for McClellan to advance. When the Yankees made no effort to do so, Johnston understood that operations would soon be suspended for the winter and ordered his men to construct winter quarters behind their Centreville lines. Most of the men banded together in small groups and built log huts 15 to 20 feet square, each housing 8

A political cartoon makes sport of the period of inactivity in both Union and Confederate armies following the battle of Bull Run.

to 10 men. The huts, which were chinked with dirt and mud and were equipped with makeshift chimneys or even stone fireplaces, proved to be good protection from the cold weather that soon set in.

The morale of the troops was reasonably good during that first winter of the war. Most of the men had more than enough warm clothing, and food supplies (except fresh fruits and vegetables) were sufficient, if not always tasty. The principal enemy the troops had to face that winter was not the Yankees, but disease. The gathering of so many men from different states, as well as unsanitary camps and the crowded huts, made Johnston's soldiers vulnerable to a host of diseases. First there were colds, jaundice, and diarrhea, then typhoid fever and pneumonia. There were even serious outbreaks of the measles, since many of the men—particularly those from farms and country villages—had never been exposed to the disease that most of their city-born comrades had encountered during childhood. A private in one Virginia battery wrote home that it seemed like everyone in his unit was sick with some disease or another. His battery had about 100 men on its rolls, of whom 24 were absent in the hospital or on sick leave, and an equal number were sick in camp.

Conditions were much the same for the Union soldiers encamped twenty-some miles away near Washington. The Yankee soldiers preferred smaller huts than their Confederate counterparts, as one chaplain described: "The model pattern of structure is after this fashion. A log cabin about seven feet square, just the size of a tent, is erected about four feet high. On top of this, the tent is set and securely fastened down...The openings between the logs are chinked with mortar made from the red siliceous earth beneath our encampment, with the addition of a little straw...in order to give consistence. In most, a regular cabin door is made...To some, the entrance is effected by climbing over the four feet wall...Some have procured small sheet iron stoves. The larger portion, however, have followed the model of the pioneer, having an outside chimney constructed of clay, straw and sticks. A few, despising all this effeminacy, are braving the changes of weather without any place for fire." Disease was also rife in the Union camps, and typhoid struck even General McClellan and his chief of staff.

During the winter Johnston had two important organizational problems to deal with in his army. One concerned an October 1861 directive from the War Department that his brigades should be reorganized so that all the units in each brigade would be from the same state. The directive was intended to increase morale, but did not win Johnston's approval because it would break up units that were very accustomed to working together and would necessitate a rearranging of his units and commanders. For these reasons he avoided complying with the directive, and it would not be carried out until after the battle of Antietam, over a year after it was issued.

Johnston's second problem concerned the fact that more than half of his men were due to go home in the spring. Most of his troops had enlisted in the rush of patriotism that had swept the newly created Confederacy in April and May of 1861. However, because few expected the war to last very long, many of the troops had enlisted for only 12 months service. The Confederate congress attempted to address the problem by enacting the Bounty and Furlough Act, which was passed on 1 December 1861, to take effect on 1 January 1862. The law promised a $50 bounty and a 60 day furlough to all 12 month volunteers who would reenlist. Reenlisted soldiers would be given the choice to remain with their present companies or to transfer to any other company in any branch of the service. Another provision allowed the men of reorganized companies and regiments to elect their officers democratically.

Johnston objected strongly to the law, particularly the democratic election of officers, and argued that it would ruin the army's efficiency. However, he found that he had no choice but to accept the measure, and he announced it to the army on 4 February 1862. He did, though, add a provision that the number of men allowed to go on furlough would be limited to 20 percent of each unit. This regulation did not please many of the men, but most eventually did end up reenlisting. This meant that Johnston would have to see to the reorganization of his regiments—and the election of new officers—during the midst of the coming spring campaign.

Johnston met with President Davis and his cabinet in Richmond on 20 February to discuss his options for the coming campaign. It is difficult today to determine what the result of this meeting was. Johnston later claimed that he argued for permission to withdraw the army to a new position south of Centreville. Davis wrote later that Johnston requested rein-

President of the Confederacy,
Jefferson Davis.

forcements in order to conduct an offensive, and that the general was not prepared to conduct a withdrawal because he had scouted the terrain to his rear. The only decision the two principals later agreed that was made at their conference was that Johnston would prepare his army for action by sending all his heavy guns, surplus supplies and baggage to the rear "so as to be able to advance or retreat as occasion might require."

Johnston returned to Centreville with the impression, mistaken or not, that he had Davis' permission to withdraw to the south. Increasing enemy pressure on both his flanks caused him growing concern, and he set about at once to begin removing the huge amount of stores collected at Centreville. This process was a painfully slow one because of a lack of road transport, the muddy conditions of the roads, and a lack of cooperation from railroad officials. There was only one railroad line available, the Orange & Alexandria, and it was operated by civilian authorities who failed to respond to his requests for engines and cars.

Johnston became more and more anxious as the days

passed, and by 7 March felt that he had no choice but to order a withdrawal. Large amounts of supplies that could not be moved were ordered to be burned, and a number of heavy guns had to be thrown into the Potomac because of a lack of transport. This waste of supplies and equipment particularly angered President Davis, who was not aware of Johnston's withdrawal until the army reached the Rappahannock River on the 11th. Johnston set up his headquarters at Rappahannock Station after linking up with Holmes' command at Fredericksburg. The new line was well suited to meeting any Federal land advance from Washington, but Johnston soon became concerned about possible enemy movement against Richmond from the east or southeast. For this reason he withdrew most of his men to a line slightly closer to Richmond, behind the upper Rapidan River. One infantry division and Stuart's cavalry were left as an advance guard along the upper Rappahannock, and Holmes' command was ordered to remain at Fredericksburg. Johnston then waited to see what McClellan's strategy would be.

On 13 March 1862 occurred a significant but little noted event—President Davis recalled General Robert E. Lee from Georgia to become his personal military advisor. The effect of this appointment would be profound on the course of the Peninsula campaign, indeed of the entire war.

Songs

Some of the most poignant songs of the Civil War were written during the winter of 1861-1862, when the jubilant optimism of the war's first months was dampened by the dullness of camp life and frequent deaths from disease.

Marching Along was written by William B. Bradbury, and expresses the North's confidence in its cause and in General George B. McClellan:

"Marching along, we are marching along,
Gird on the armor, we are marching along;
God is our strength, and the Union's our song,
With courage and faith we are marching along.
The foe is before us in battle array,
But let us not waver, or turn from the way;
McClellan's our leader, he's gallant and strong,
For home and country we are marching along."

The newspaper headline *All Quiet on the Potomac* was the inspiration for this song published in Baltimore in 1863. The words were by Mrs. Ethel Lynn Beers, and the music was by John Hill Hewett. The song reflects on the misfortune of soldiers torn from their families and reminds us that the death of a soldier on the picket line or in camp from disease was just as tragic as a casualty in battle:

"All quiet on the Potomac tonight,"
    Except here and there a stray picket
Is shot as he walks on his beat to and fro,
    By a rifleman hid in the thicket;
'Tis nothing! a private or two now and then,
    Will not count in the news of the battle,
Not an officer lost! only one of the men,
    Moaning out all alone the death rattle.

All quiet on the Potomac to-night!
    Where the soldiers lie peacefully dreaming;
And their tents in the rays of the clear autumn moon,
    And the light of their camp-fires are gleaming.
A tremulous sigh, as a gentle night-wind
    Through the forest leaves slowly is creeping;

While the stars up above, with their glittering eyes,
    Keep guard o'er the army sleeping.

There's only the sound of the lone sentry's tread,
    As he tramps from the rock to the fountain,
And thinks of the two on the low trundel bed,
    Far away, in the cot on the mountain.
His musket falls slack, his face, dark and grim,
    Grows gentle with memories tender,
As he mutters a prayer for the children asleep,
    And their mother—"may heaven defend her!"

The moon seems to shine forth as brightly as then—
    That night, when the love, yet unspoken,
Leaped up to his lips, and when low-murmured vows
    Were pledged ever to be unbroken.
Then drawing his sleeve roughly over his eyes,
    He dashes off the tears that are welling;
And gathers the gun closer up to his breast,
    As if to keep down his heart's swelling.

He passes the fountain, the blasted pine-tree,
    And his footstep is lagging and weary;
Yet onward he goes, through the broad belt of light,
    Towards the shades of the forest so dreary.
Hark! was it the night-wind that rustled the leaves?
    Was it the moonlight so wondrously flashing?
It looked like a rifle: "Ha! Mary, good-bye!"
    And his life-blood is ebbing and splashing.
"All quiet along the Potomac to-night!"
    No sound save the rush of the river;
While soft falls the dew on the face of the dead,
    And the picket's off duty forever.

The North's most popular wartime song was perhaps *Battle Hymn of the Republic*. The words were written by Julia Ward Howe, a Boston abolitionist, during a visit to the Union army's camps near Washington in the fall of 1861. She was greatly impressed by the campfires of the soldiers and their divine mission, and went home with the camp song *John Brown's Body* ringing in her ears. When one of her friends remarked that the tune needed better lyrics, Miss Howe wrote down her poem that began "Mine eyes have seen the glory of the coming of the Lord." The song was published in Boston

in 1862. Curiously, the original music to the song was written by a
Southerner, William Steffe.

Mine eyes have seen the glory of the coming of the Lord!
He is trampling out the vintage where the grapes of wrath are
  stored;
He hath loosed the fateful lightning of His terrible swift
  sword;
His truth is marching on.

(Chorus)
Glory! Glory Hallelujah!
Glory! Glory Hallelujah!
Glory! Glory Hallelujah!
His truth is marching on.

I have seen Him in the watch-fires of a hundred circling
  camps,
They have builded Him an altar in the evening dews and
  damps;
I can read His righteous sentence by the dim and flaring
  lamps:
His day is marching on.
(Chorus)

I have read a fiery gospel writ in burnished rows of steel:
"As ye deal with my contemners, so with you my grace shall
  deal;
Let the hero born of woman crush the serpent with His heel,
Since God is marching on."
(Chorus)

He has sounded forth the trumpet that shall never call retreat;
He is sifting out the hearts of men before His judgement seat:
Oh, be swift, my soul, to answer Him! be jubilant my feet!
Our God is marching on.
(Chorus)

In the beauty of the lilies Christ was born across the sea,
With a glory in his bosom that transfigures you and me;
As he died to make men holy, let us die to make men free,
While God is marching on.
(Chorus)

Regimental Organization and Strengths

The typical Civil War infantry regiment on both sides consisted of 10 companies (letters "A" through "K" but with no "I") of 101 men each (see chart A) and a regimental headquarters of 15 men (see chart B), giving the unit a total strength of 1,025. No regiment ever entered action with this many men, as attrition from disease, desertion and other causes took their toll soon after regiments were sworn in. Battle losses further decreased the units' strengths noticeably, and neither side made a serious effort to restore their regiments to full strength. The Confederates, at least, tried to channel new recruits and draftees into veteran regiments in order to retain unit continuity and efficiency. The Federal armies suffered from the fact that old regiments were literally permitted to wither away while new ones were constantly being raised. This permitted the state governors to appoint a steady flow of new colonels, but did not maintain the combat efficiency of regiments, thereby giving the Confederates a distinct organizational advantage until the last year of the war (see chart C). Altogether the South enlisted approximately 750 regiments, while the North had 2,060 regiments—1,708 infantry, 272 cavalry, and 78 artillery. Artillery regiments never fought as a unit, but in detached companies (batteries) that had a strength of up to 150 men. Cavalry regiments usually had 12 companies each, and some U.S. Regular infantry regiments had as many as 24 companies in two battalions.

A. COMPANY FORMATION
1 Captain
1 First Lieutenant
1 Second Lieutenant
1 First Sergeant
4 Sergeants
8 Corporals
2 Musicians
1 Wagoner
82 Privates
101

B. REGIMENTAL FIELD AND STAFF

1 Colonel
1 Lieutenant Colonel
1 Major
1 Adjutant
1 Quartermaster
1 Surgeon
2 Assistant Surgeons
1 Chaplain
1 Sergeant Major
1 Quartermaster Sergeant
1 Commissary Sergeant
1 Hospital Steward
<u>2 Principal Musicians</u>
15

C. Average Regimental Strength in Selected Civil War Battles

Engagement	Date	North	South
First Bull Run	21 July 61	665	725
Shiloh	6-7 April 62	545	475
Seven Days	25 June-1 July 62	575	430
Second Bull Run	29-30 August 62	460	310
Antietam	17 September 62	345	165
Fredericksburg	13 December 62	415	350
Chancellorsville	1-4 May 63	415	400
Gettysburg	1-3 July 63	310	350
Chickamauga	19-20 September 63	395	375
Wilderness	5-7 May 64	420	320
Atlanta	20-28 July 64	295	285
Appomattox	29 March-9 April 65	355	210

Figures are rough averages, based on incomplete information. Of particular interest is the decline experienced during periods of intensive movement and combat, such as Second Bull Run and Antietam, in August and September of 1862, and Chancellorsville and Gettysburg in May, June, and July of 1863. Sources: Livermore, *Numbers and Losses in the Civil War, Battles and Leaders of the Civil War, The Official Records of the War of the Rebellion*, and Boatner, *The Civil War Dictionary*.

Robert E. Lee's Family

Robert E. Lee's family traced its beginnings to a Norman knight named Reyner de Lea, who in the 1100's lived near Shrewsbury, located in Shropshire in western England close to the border with Wales. De Lea's original home was replaced in 1571 by a newer Lea Hall, which is still standing. The Lee family crest was surmounted by a squirrel nibbling an acorn and had the appropriate motto "Non Incautus Futuri" ("Not Unmindful of the Future")

The progenitor of the Lee line in America was Richard Lee, who was born in Shropshire in the early 1600's. He arrived in Jamestown in 1649 or 1650, and 10 years later was named secretary of state of Virginia. Richard steadily expanded his land holdings in the tidewater district, and became one of the richest men in the colony before he died in 1664. The Lee family thrived and spread, as each member produced a large family. Richard's second son, Richard (1646-1714) had a son named Henry (1691-1747), who also had a son named Henry (1729-1787), who was the father of a third Henry better known as "Light Horse Harry" (1756-1818), the noted Revolutionary war officer. "Light Horse Harry" was the father of Robert Edward Lee (1807-1870)

Young Robert hardly knew his father, as "Light Horse Harry" had financial problems and had to leave the country in 1813 in voluntary exile in order to escape his creditors. Of his two brothers, two sisters, one half-brother and one half-sister, Robert was closest to his older brother Sydney (1802-1869), who attended the Naval Academy in Annapolis and later became an officer in the Confederate navy. Robert was perhaps closest of all to his mother, Ann Hill Carter Lee (1773-1829). She was ill for most of her later years, and Lee patiently and selflessly nursed her whenever he was home. In many ways, his wife Mary Anne Custis Lee (1808-1873) was similar to his mother, as Mary was also an invalid for most of her later years; she suffered so much from arthritis that she was usually confined to a wheelchair. Lee took her affliction stoically, and remained devoted to her to the end. He seldom socialized himself in his later years, and was thought by his biographers to prefer the intellectual companionship of women to that of men.

Robert and Mary Lee had seven children in the 16 years from 1832 to 1846. Altogether there were four daughters and three sons. Curiously, none of the four daughters ever married. Their names were Mary Custis (born in 1835), Annie (1839-1862), Agnes, and Mildred (born in 1846).

The general's oldest child and first son was named George Washington Custis after the boy's mother's family. He was born in

1832 at Fort Monroe, Virginia, while his father was on duty there. Known as "Custis," the lad followed in his father's footsteps and entered West Point in 1850. He graduated first in the class of 1854 and became a first lieutenant of Engineers, remaining in the army until he resigned in the crisis of 1861. Custis' initial Confederate appointment was also in the engineers. Later he became a valued member of President Jefferson Davis' staff, rising to the rank of major general in 1864. Custis had a yearning for field command, but fought only briefly as commander of a makeshift regiment at Sailor's Creek just before the end of the war. After the war he taught engineering at the Virginia Military Institute until his father died in 1870. He was then named president of Washington and Lee College, so succeeding his father; reportedly he was named to the post because the school's trustees did not want to move his invalid mother out of her home on campus. Custis served the school well until forced by ill health to resign in 1897. He lived out his last days at "Ravensworth," his brother Rooney's former estate in Fairfax. Custis died in 1913, a bachelor to the end. He was a handsome, competent man who could never quite escape the shadow of his illustrious father and his more successful brother Rooney.

General Lee's third child and second son was named William Henry Fitzhugh, known to the family as "Rooney." He was born at Arlington, his mother's family estate,

in 1837. Rooney chose to attend Harvard rather than West Point, but ended up choosing the army as a career when he volunteered to join the Regular Army as a second lieutenant of infantry in 1857. In 1861 he became a captain in the Confederate cavalry, and by the next year rose to the rank of colonel of the 9th Virginia Cavalry. Soon thereafter he was named brigadier general, and became one of Jeb Stuart's mainstays as a brigade commander. He was brave in the saddle, and was wounded at South Mountain and again at Brandy Station. While recovering from the second wound, he was captured by the Yankees and held in prison until exchanged in March 1864. On 23 April 1864, Rooney was appointed Major General, at age 36 the youngest officer in the Confederate army to hold that rank. For a time in late 1864 he commanded the army's cavalry corps, and during the final retreat from Richmond in 1865 was second-in-command of his father's army. Following the war he rebuilt his home near Richmond, named "White House," which had been destroyed by the Federals on 29 June 1862 during their retreat from Richmond during the Peninsula Campaign. He also vainly attempted to regain possession of his parents' home at Arlington, which had been in government hands since 1861. The courts eventually decided in favor of the Lee family, but by then the estate was no longer useable because it had been converted into a cemetery. Rooney finally decided to accept a cash settlement for the property. In the post-war years he led a successful life, serving as president of the Virginia Agricultural Society and also as a state senator and then representative in Richmond. He died in 1891 and is buried in the Lee family mausoleum at Washington and Lee University in Lexington. He was married and had two sons.

The sixth child and third son of General Lee was named Robert Edward Junior. He was born at Arlington in 1843, and had fond memories of the formative years he lived at West Point when his father was Commandant there from 1852 to 1855. General Lee was a caring and supportive father, but also a demanding one, as this anecdote from Robert Jr. relates: "Sitting down by me, he would show me how to overcome a hard sentence in my Latin reader or a difficult sum in arithmetic, not by giving me the translation of the troublesome sentence or the answer to the sum, but by showing me, step by step, the way to the right solutions...When I was able to bring home a good report from my teacher, he was greatly pleased, but he always insisted that I should get the 'maximum', that he would never be perfectly satisfied with less. My father was the most punctual man I ever knew...He expected all of us to be the same and taught us the use and necessity of forming such habits."

Robert Jr. was a student at the University of Virginia when the war broke out in 1861, and was anxious to enlist. His father, however, did not encourage him to do so, since there were plenty of soldiers available and the additional education, Lee felt, would do the lad good. Robert Sr. finally gave in that winter and permitted young "Bob" to enlist in the 1st Rockbridge Artillery in March of 1862. Later that year Bob accepted a commission as lieutenant of cavalry, and he served the rest of the war as an aide to his brother Rooney. After the war he was a farmer in King William County and then a businessman in Washington D.C. He died in 1914 and is also buried in the Lee family mausoleum in Lexington. Bob was married and had two daughters. He had a very pleasant personality and closely resembled his father in appearance. He was the author of *Recollections and Letters of General Robert E. Lee*, a very personal and informative book published in 1904.

Fitzhugh Lee, son of Robert E. Lee's older brother Sydney, was yet another famous general during the war. He was born in 1835 and graduated from West Point in 1856. After being badly wounded in the Indian Wars, Fitzhugh joined the Confederate service as a lieutenant in 1861. He served as a staff officer during the Peninsula Campaign. After the close of the campaign he was appointed a brigadier general of cavalry, and found his fame there as another of Jeb Stuart's most reliable brigade commanders. In late 1863 he was made a major general and led a division until he was badly wounded at Third Winchester. He did not recover until the war was almost over, when he briefly led his uncle's cavalry corps. Fitzhugh had a very successful post-war career that included service as governor of Virginia from 1885 to 1889 and as consul-general in Havana from 1896-1898. He was appointed a major general of United States Volunteers during the war with Spain, much to the delight of the numerous ex-Confederates who served with him. He died in 1905.

A number of other "Lee's" served in both the Union and Confederate armies during the war, but none were close relatives to the commander of the Army of Northern Virginia. Stephen D. Lee (1833-1908) was a distant relative who was born in Charleston, South Carolina, and served as a lieutenant general in the Confederacy's western theater. Edwin G. Lee (1835-1870) was for a time colonel of the 33rd Virginia Infantry, but was not a close relative of Robert E. Lee. Union cavalry general Albert L. Lee (1834-1907) was the highest ranking of the northern Lee's in the war, none of whom were related to the Confederate commander-in-chief. Others included Brevet Brigadier Generals Edwin M. Lee of New Jersey and Michigan, Horace C. Lee of Massachusetts, and John C. Lee of Ohio.

CHAPTER III

The Campaign Begins

*U*nion General George B. McClellan's labored plans for a water-borne movement to Urbanna were upset in early March 1862 by two unexpected events. The first concerned the Confederate ironclad *Virginia* (also known as the *Merrimac*). Northern authorities were aware that the Confederates were constructing an ironclad at Norfolk, but they underestimated its significance and power (see sidebar). McClellan had sketched out plans to capture Norfolk and size the uncompleted vessel, but he did not give the movement priority and dallied at finalizing his plans. Thus McClellan and all of Washington were astounded when they heard that the *Virginia* had suddenly appeared on 8 March and destroyed two of the navy's largest wooden warships at Hampton Roads. Everyone was well aware that the enemy ironclad might wreck the Union blockading fleet and then be able to roam at will up and down the coast, destroying commerce and threatening every Northern seaport. McClellan also quickly realized that there was no way he could move his army by water to eastern Virginia in the face of a strong and unrestrained enemy ironclad. Fortunately for McClellan, the *Virginia* crisis subsided as quickly as it had arisen. The Union *Monitor* reached Hampton Roads on 8 March and then fought the *Virginia* to a draw. The Confederate warship had to retire to Norfolk for repairs, and would in the future be kept in check by the *Monitor*.

While McClellan was evaluating the disturbing news

49

The *Monitor* and the *Virginia*

The famous duel between the Union *Monitor* and the Confederate *Virginia* (a.k.a. *Merrimac*)—the first battle in history between ironclad warships—formed more than an interesting sideshow to the Peninsula Campaign. The *Virginia* was completed and prepared for action in early March 1862, and was ready to break the Union blockade and threaten all Federal shipping on the East coast. Union General George B. McClellan knew that if the *Virginia* were on the loose, he would be unable to transport his army by water from Washington to Urbanna or Fort Monroe as his campaign plan required. The sudden appearance of the *Monitor* on 9 March and that warship's ability to neutralize the *Virginia* made McClellan's seaborne operation and the ensuing Peninsula campaign possible.

The *Virginia* had its origins with the U.S.S. *Merrimack,* a screw steamer that had been burned and scuttled when the Unionists abandoned the Gosport Navy Yard at Norfolk on 21 April 1861. The Confederates decided to raise the *Merrimack* and use her hull as the base for an ironclad to be called the *Virginia.* The sides of the *Virginia* consisted of four inches of iron bars laid on top of twenty-two inches of oak, all set at a 35 degree angle. She was armed with 10 heavy guns (six 9-inch smoothbore Dahlgrens, two 7-inch rifled guns and

two 8-inch rifled guns) and had a four-foot-long iron ram at the prow. The warship, which was not the first ironclad built during the war (a fair number were already operating in the war's western theater) carried a crew of 350 men, all under the command of Commodore Franklin Buchanan. Her only weakness was her heavy draught (22 feet) and slow speed (4 knots); it took the ship 30 minutes just to turn around.

The *Virginia* was finished on 5 March and sailed three days later into Hampton Roads to attack the Union blockading fleet stationed there. The attack began at 1400 on 8 March and marked the end of the era of wooden warships. The *Virginia* was impervious to Union cannon shots and rammed the 30 gun U.S.S. *Cumberland.* It then forced the 50 gun U.S.S. *Congress* to run aground, and a number of smaller vessels also ran aground while trying to escape. The warship U.S.S. *Minnesota* escaped only because she was in water too shallow for the *Virginia* to enter. The Confederate ship retired at 1700 after three hours of action, with plans to return the next day to finish off the *Minnesota* and the rest of the Union fleet that did not run away. Southern casualties had amounted to only 21 men, including Commodore Buchanan, who was wounded. (The commodore's brother, McKean Buchanan, was a

Union paymaster on the *Congress* and was killed during the battle.)

When the *Virginia* returned to Hampton Roads the next morning, her crew was surprised to see a strange looking Union ironclad ready to defend the grounded *Minnesota*. This was the *Monitor*, a uniquely designed warship that was aptly described at the time as a "cheese box on a raft." She was 172 feet long (90 feet shorter than the *Virginia*) and had a draught of only 10 and one-half feet. The ship carried only two cannons (11-inch Dahlgren smoothbores) that were mounted on opposite sides of an ingenious revolving turret. The turret was nine feet high, and covered with eight inches of iron plates; the rest of the boat above water was protected by four and one-half inches of armor plating. The warship was designed by inventor John Ericcson and took just three months to build. She was commissioned on 25 February and left New York on 6 March for Hampton Roads carrying a crew of 58 men under the command of Lieutenant J. L. Worden.

The *Monitor* arrived at Hampton Roads on the evening of 8 March just in time to save what was left of the Union fleet. Her historic encounter with the *Virginia* began at 0900 on 9 March. The two ironclads pummeled each other for about four hours and neither was able to do much more than dent the other's armor. The battle ended when the *Virginia* returned to Norfolk; the *Monitor* was unable to follow because a lucky shot from her foe had struck her pilot house and blinded Lieutenant Worden.

The two ironclads played cat and mouse with each other several times in the ensuing month but did not fight another engagement. The *Virginia* continued to guard the James River, effectively prohibiting the Union warships from approaching Richmond. The *Monitor*, on the other hand, was able to keep the *Virginia* from proceeding up the coast from Norfolk. The impasse ended on 9 May when the Confederate evacuation of Yorktown compelled Major General Benjamin Huger to abandon Norfolk. Since the *Virginia* had too deep a draught to enable her to escape up the James, the Confederates had no choice but to blow her up in order to keep her out of Union hands.

The *Monitor* was involved in the unsuccessful Union attack on Drewry's Bluff on the James River below Richmond on 15 May 1862. She did not see action again afterwards. On 31 December 1862 she sank in a gale off of Cape Hatteras while being towed south for action farther down the coast. Four officers and twelve men were lost with her. The remains of the *Monitor* were found in 1973 in 220 feet of water. The wreck is in bad shape because it was mistaken for a German submarine and was bombed with depth charges by our coastal defenders during World War II. Today opinion is divided whether to salvage the wreck or leave it as a memorial to the men who died with the warship.

about the *Virginia*'s appearance, equally disconcerting reports began to come in on 9 March that the Confederate army had vanished from its lines along the Potomac and its camp at Centreville. General Banks, commander on the upper Potomac, reported the enemy to be withdrawing from his front, and scouts all along the lower Potomac reported that the Confederates had destroyed or removed all their batteries. Most astounding of all was the claim by a contraband slave that the Confederates had abandoned Manassas and Centreville.

This unexpected news took McClellan totally by surprise. He decided that night to mobilize his army and send it in pursuit of Johnston, with the hope of catching a part of the Confederate army out in the open away from its fortifications. On the morning of 10 March over 100,000 Federal soldiers came streaming out of Washington in a steady rain, eager to take the war to the enemy at long last. They were prepared to fight, but their advance was too slow and Johnston had too much of a head start to be caught. McClellan later defended himself for letting Johnston cleanly escape by explaining that his advance was also conducted "to break up the winter camps, give the troops a little experience in marching and bivouac before leaving the old base of supplies, to test the transportation arrangements and get rid of impedimenta, and thus prepare things for the movement to the Peninsula." This explanation is clearly a weak excuse for the fact that Johnston clearly stole a march on McClellan. Some of the Yankee soldiers vented their frustration at not being able to catch the enemy by looting many old buildings in Fairfax, including the courthouse, where numerous old and historical records were wantonly destroyed.

McClellan's advance troops were astonished at the amount of equipment and supplies the Confederates had destroyed or left behind, some of which was still burning. As McClellan set up quarters in what was left of Fairfax, the troops readily made themselves at home in the abandoned

The formidable C.S.S. Virginia prepares to unload a broadside against the innovative U.S.S. Monitor. Both warships bombarded each other to a stalemate in a four-hour battle which marked the first contest between ironclads.

Confederate winter camps. McClellan did not plan for an immediate advance beyond Centreville, since he first needed to ascertain where Johnston was establishing his new position. He thought that it was glorious to finally occupy Manassas, and many of his men agreed. However, they were sombered by visits to the battlefield of Bull Run and the sight of the bones of partially buried Union casualties from the July 1861 battle.

McClellan tried to claim credit for "capturing" Manassas by asserting that the Confederates knew that he was preparing to advance and were afraid to face him. This was largely true, since Johnston had only about 48,000 men to face him (and not the 70,000 to 102,000 McClellan believed he had). The argument, however, did not impress the authorities in Washington, many of whom were disappointed that Johnston had escaped without a fight. McClellan was especially embarrassed by the fact that the Confederate defenses at Centreville were not as strong as he thought. The large number of wooden "Quaker" guns were of particular interest to critical newspaper reporters.

Criticism of McClellan quickly mounted in Washington, and some officials urged that he be replaced before he could begin his spring campaign. Lincoln felt their pressure, but he was not prepared to fire McClellan, perhaps because there was no suitable replacement at hand. Instead, Lincoln felt that it was in the best interest of the country to relieve McClellan of his duties as commander-in-chief in order to permit him to use all his energy to lead the *Army of the Potomac* to victory. Presidential War Order Number 3, dated 11 March 1862, stated as follows: "Major General McClellan having personally taken the field at the head of the *Army of the Potomac*, until otherwise ordered he is relieved from the command of the other military departments, he retaining command of the Department of the Potomac." The same directive gave overall command in the war's western theater to General Henry Halleck. Unfortunately, Lincoln chose not to appoint a successor to McClellan as the army's head general. Instead, he directed that all the department heads should report directly to the secretary of war. Apparently Lincoln envisioned that the war could be successfully directed by himself and Secretary Stanton, neither of whom were professionally trained soldiers. Lincoln would soon discover that this was not a wise decision.

McClellan was taken aback by his demotion, and considered it a slap in the face to learn of it through the newspapers before the actual orders reached him from Washington. He was in better spirits when he received reassurance from Lincoln that he would be given free reins to direct the *Army of the Potomac*. This led the beleaguered general to the belief that the president was his "strongest friend", protecting him from the "rascals" in Washington who were trying to undermine him. He optimistically hoped to regain command of all the Union armies once he had successfully completed his drive on Richmond.

Confirmed at least in his role as army commander, Mc-

Clellan summoned his four corps commanders to a conference at his Fairfax headquarters on 13 March. By then he had learned that Johnston had fallen back to a new line along the Rapidan. This information put him in a quandary. Johnston's new position gave the Confederate army access to a direct railroad line from Fredericksburg to Richmond, so rendering McClellan's Urbanna plan obsolete.

McClellan would gain no advantage by landing at Urbanna, which was approximately the same distance from Richmond as Fredericksburg. A logical alternative for McClellan would have been to abandon his plans to move by water and instead conduct a direct attack on Culpeper or Fredericksburg before the Confederates had time to strengthen their lines and construct fortifications. McClellan, however, was reluctant to abandon all the effort he had spent to plan the Urbanna move. After much lobbying and cajoling he had finally convinced the navy to cooperate fully with the expedition, and barges and naval transport were already being gathered in large numbers at Washington.

The plan McClellan presented to his corps commanders at Fairfax was a modified version of the Urbanna plan. Instead of transporting the army by water to Urbanna, he would instead convey it to Fort Monroe, at the tip of the Peninsula formed by the York and James Rivers. A rapid advance past Williamsburg might catch the Confederates unawares and offered the possibility of striking Richmond from its unprotected southern side. The plan's only weakness was the threat posed by the *Virginia*, but McClellan received reassurance from the navy that the powerful Confederate ironclad could be held neutralized.

McClellan presented his new plan thoroughly and forcefully. He discussed the merits of such a line of advance versus a move on the Rapidan line, and reviewed the naval support and water transportation he had arranged. His generals unanimously agreed to the plan, mostly because, as one witness put it, "they knew that general McClellan had made up his mind to move to the Peninsula." There was some disagreement, however, on how many men should be left in northern Virginia to cover the Washington defenses. Sumner thought that 40,000 should be left, while the other three corps commanders argued that 25,000 would be sufficient. Lastly, it should be noted that McClellan accepted the recommendation of his top advisers that the army should advance at once against Johnston's Rapidan line if for any reason the seaborne movement could not be carried out.

McClellan notified President Lincoln at once of the outcome of his war council, and Lincoln promptly replied, via Stanton, that he made "no objection" to the plans, as long as the following three considerations were met: that Washington would be "entirely secure"; that Manassas Junction would be closely guarded so that the Confederates could not reoccupy it; and that the army would move "at once" in pursuit of the enemy by any route.

McClellan devoted his attention eagerly and energetically to the operation once it got underway. On 15 March he ordered most of the troops to return to their old camps outside Washington; a portion of Sumner's corps was left behind to garrison Manassas. Lest the men become despondent about returning to Washington, he announced to them that they were on the eve of the war's decisive campaign. His address, though Napoleonic in tone, was well received by his troops, who still trusted their commander despite what the newspapers were saying: "I am to watch over you as a parent over his children; and you know that your general loves you from the depths of his heart. It shall be my care, as it has ever been, to gain success with the least possible loss...I shall demand of you great, heroic exertions, rapid and long marches, desperate combats, privations perhaps. We will share all these together, and when this sad war is over we will return to our homes, and feel that we can ask no higher honor than the proud consciousness that we belonged to the Army of the Potomac."

It was McClellan's desire to move the army to Fort Monroe as quickly as possible in order to gain an advantage on the enemy. Johnston's unexpected withdrawal from Centreville and the Union army's foray to Manassas delayed his schedule for a few days. On the 13th and 14th, following final approval of his campaign plans, he sent out a flurry of telegrams in order to have everything ready to go as soon as he and his troops arrived back in Washington. He ordered all the transports to be gathered at once at Alexandria. Because the army and navy did not own many small vessels in this theater, almost all the transports used in the campaign had to be chartered from businesses and individuals. Records show that some 113 steamers were contracted at an average cost of $215.10 per day, along with 188 schooners at $24.45 per day and 88 barges at $14.27 per day. Altogether the maneuver would involve over 400 vessels, by far the largest combined arms operation the nation had ever attempted.

All did not go smoothly at first. McClellan was dismayed to learn that the naval supporting craft needed additional time to reach the rendezvous from their base at Annapolis. He became still more annoyed when he found on reaching Alexandria that transports for only 25,000 men were ready, despite the fact that he had been promised vessels for twice that many men. He nevertheless began the movement at once, and Hamilton's division of Heintzelman's corps began embarking on the 17th. Porter's division left five days later, whereupon the next troops in line had to wait for the transports to make the return trip and pick them up.

The voyage from Alexandria to Fort Monroe, which usually took two or three days, was a great adventure for the troops, most of whom had never been at sea before. The men were at first impressed by the sight of Mount Vernon and George Washington's tomb, which were clearly visible from the river. "After passing Mount Vernon," one soldier wrote, "nothing of special interest was seen except the broad expanse of waters of this magnificent stream. A few large man-sions, a few inferior houses, and now and then a little hamlet, appeared on the banks." After traversing the upper waters of Chesapeake Bay, the convoys sailed up to Fort Monroe, which was most impressive and appeared to some troops to be one of the strongest fortifications in the world. When the weather was good, the transports lined up to use the limited dock space near the fort. Some units, such as the *63rd Pennsylvania*, had the misfortune to arrive during foul weather: "The sea became very rough and we had to land when the waves were breaking in great billows over the beach. The vessels dashed against each other, cables were broken, and steamers full of men drifted helplessly from the docks. In the most unpitying storm we landed and gathered in shivering bands on the shore."

Once ashore, the men were marched a couple miles to the west to an encampment near the town of Hampton, a once beautiful place that had been burned to the ground when the Confederates evacuated the area earlier in the war. One impressed soldier noted that "dense masses of infantry, long trains of artillery, and thousands of cavalry, with unnumbered army wagons and mules were intermingled in grand confusion along the shore. The neighing of horses, the braying of mules, and the sound of many voices mingled in one grand inharmonious concert." Altogether it would take a total of 20 days for McClellan's vast army, its equipment and supplies to be conveyed to Fort Monroe. John Tucker, the assistant secretary of war, calculated that the navy transported a total of 121,500 men, 14,592 animals, 1,150 wagons, 44 batteries, and 14 ambulances, as well as pontoon bridges, telegraphic materials, and vast quantities of other equipment. To his knowledge, no soldiers were lost during the operation. The only casualties reported were eight mules and nine barges lost in a gale a few miles from Fort Monroe.

McClellan himself embarked for Fort Monroe on 1 April in the midst of a growing controversy with Lincoln and the War Department over the number of troops to be left behind to guard Washington. McClellan had planned to shift most of Nathaniel Banks' corps to the Washington area to meet the promise he had made to keep Washington well guarded. This plan was upset on 23 March when "Stonewall" Jackson unexpectedly attacked a portion of Banks' command at Kernstown, outside of Winchester. Jackson was defeated at the battle, but the audaciousness of his attack convinced President Lincoln that the Confederates had many more troops in the Valley than they actually did. As a result, Lincoln made McClellan pledge to keep Banks in the Valley until Jackson was driven back. This meant that McClellan had to use other troops to replace Banks as the covering force for Washington. At the end of the month McClellan's strength was further sapped when Lincoln detached Blenker's "German" division from the *Army of the Potomac* and reassigned it to Major General John Fremont's newly created department in the western Virginia mountains.

Just before he left for Fort Monroe, McClellan filed a strength report with the War Department showing that he had left 18,000 men in the Washington garrison and another 55,000 in the covering force. The total of 73,000 was quite sufficient to guard the capital, as he had promised. Lincoln and Stanton, however, were not at all pleased to discover that McClellan's numbers were faulty and deceptive. He included Banks' command as the bulk of the covering force, even though these troops were at least 75 miles west of the capital. He also overestimated the strength of Wadsworth's Washington garrison by 3,000 men, and further erred in his estimation by counting one of Banks' brigades and four of Wadsworth's regiments twice in his tally. Lincoln and Stanton were even more annoyed when they found that McClellan included 3,500 fresh troops still in Pennsylvania as part of the Washington garrison. All this meant that McClellan had left only 26,700 men at Washington and Manassas, and many of these troops were too green to be relied on. When the president understood this, "he was justly indignant," as one senator put it.

Jackson's Valley Campaign

McClellan's Peninsula Campaign was not the only operation being conducted in Virginia in the spring of 1862. From March through May, Confederate Major General Thomas J. "Stonewall" Jackson was conducting one of the most brilliant campaigns of the war in Virginia's fertile Shenandoah Valley. Jackson's primary objective was to draw troops and attention away from McClellan's army, and at this he succeeded admirably. The details of Jackson's campaign are too lengthy to be discussed here in detail, and may be studied in a companion volume of this series, *Jackson's Valley Campaign*, by Dr. David G. Martin.

Jackson's Valley Campaign began in March 1862 when Major General Nathaniel Banks' Union troops moved south from Harpers Ferry to occupy Winchester in order to secure the lower Shenandoah Valley before joining McClellan's *Army of the Potomac* for the pending movement to the Peninsula. Jackson, then based in the upper Valley, learned of the enemy movement and boldly marched north to attack Shields' division of Banks' force at Kernstown on 23 March. The battle was a tactical defeat for Jackson, but became a strategic victory because it drew attention to his command. The very boldness of his attack led President Lincoln and Secretary of War Stanton (who were then direct-

ing the war after McClellan was demoted from Union general in chief) to assume that Jackson had greater strength than he did. As a result, Banks was ordered to remain in the Valley and never did join McClellan's campaign. In addition, Lincoln ordered McClellan to detach another division (Blenker's) to join Fremont's Mountain Department west of the Valley. Most significantly, Lincoln's concern for the safety of Washington caused him to retain McDowell's corps for use as a covering force in front of the capital. McDowell's command was the largest corps in McClellan's army, and its absence would be sorely felt during the coming campaign.

Jackson's small force of 6,000 men was compelled to retire slowly up the Valley when Banks occupied New Market on 26 April. The complexion of the campaign changed markedly after Jackson received heavy reinforcements to raise his strength to 17,000. On 8 May he suddenly and unexpectedly struck and defeated Fremont's small army at McDowell in the Allegheny Mountains west of Staunton. Banks nevertheless thought that he could maintain control of the Valley. Based on this assurance, Lincoln detached one of Banks' divisions (Shields') and finally on 18 May yielded to McClellan's urging to allow McDowell's 30,000 men to march south to Richmond to join in McClellan's assault on the city. McClellan was so anxious to receive McDowell's command that he extended the right wing of his line (Porter's corps) along the Chickahominy north towards Hanover Junction in order to connect with McDowell's advance. (Lincoln had refused McClellan permission to bring McDowell to Richmond by water since he wanted to keep Washington covered as much as possible.) McDowell was all set to march south and believed that he could reach Richmond in four or five days after dealing with a small Confederate force that was observing him. However, his advance was delayed several days while he waited for Shields' division to come up.

McDowell never did get the opportunity to march to join McClellan at Richmond. When Jackson learned that Banks' command had been weakened, he boldly marched his vaunted "foot cavalry" down the length of the Valley and defeated Banks at Front Royal (23 May) and Winchester (25 May). These successes alarmed Lincoln and his advisors so much that they formed a complicated plan to trap and destroy the wily Confederate, who had by then advanced to the Potomac. Fremont was ordered to march on Strasburg from his base in western Virginia and link up with Shields, who was directed to return to the Valley. Their combined forces would block Jackson from escaping up the Valley while Banks closed the trap from the north. Just to be on the safe side, Lincoln countermanded McDowell's orders to march for Richmond. As a result, McDowell's large command never did reach McClellan, who had to fight the Seven Days Battles without him.

Lincoln's plan barely missed catching Jackson. By hard marching, Jackson managed to pass through Strasburg just before the trap closed. He then marched south, pursued by Fremont's army in the main Valley and by Shields' in the eastern or Luray Valley. Jackson made perfect use of local geography to exact defeats on Fremont at Cross Keys on 8 June and on Shields at Port Republic on 9 June. The Valley campaign came to a close as Jackson rested his men for a few days before joining Lee's army at Richmond in the fourth week of June.

Jackson's Valley Campaign was a remarkable success. In the space of 10 weeks he fought 5 major battles, winning 4 of them, and with 17,000 men defeated 3 small Union armies numbering some 41,000 men. His greatest success may have been the neutralizing of McDowell's 30,000 man command and preventing it from joining McClellan's attack on Richmond. McClellan could have profitably used McDowell's men at several points in the campaign—particularly to get behind the Confederate lines at Yorktown or to extend his own lines north of Richmond—but he would never enjoy their use thanks to Jackson's boldness and Lincoln's strategic errors.

McClellan's deliberate attempt to deceive Lincoln and Stanton on the number of troops he left behind to guard Washington destroyed the trust of the administration and the few parties that still had confidence in him. Stanton was so disgusted with McClellan that he began to hold interviews for someone to replace him. Lincoln decided that it was not right to change horses in midstream now that the campaign was finally underway, so he let McClellan stay on. However, he did insist that the general leave McDowell's large corps of over 30,000 men behind to help cover Washington. McClellan was greatly displeased to leave McDowell's men behind, and rightly so, because the continued absence of such a large force from the army would have a severe effect on the course of the campaign.

CHAPTER IV

Yorktown

*T*he size and scope of McClellan's naval movement to Fort Monroe caught Confederate General Joe Johnston completely by surprise. In mid-March he was still trying to form his new defensive line along the Rapidan River, which he had reached after withdrawing from Manassas and Centreville on 7 March. He felt that he did not have enough men to hold the line properly, and on the 22nd met with President Davis and Davis' new military advisor, Robert E. Lee, to discuss the problem. Davis stated that he had no new troops available, but hoped more would arrive shortly. The Confederate president was also gravely concerned about increased enemy activity in the area of New Bern, North Carolina. For this reason he could not loan Johnston any of the 12,000 men that Major General John B. Magruder had at Yorktown or any of the 13,000 troops that Major General Benjamin Huger had at Norfolk guarding the ironclad *Virginia* and its base.

Johnston was unaware of McClellan's movement for a whole week after it started. It was not until 23 March that his scouts reported seeing a continuous stream of transports moving down the Potomac. Their destination was at first uncertain, and it remained unknown until General Huger reported that 20 enemy steamers had sailed down Chesapeake Bay and landed near Fort Monroe. Even so, Davis and his advisors were uncertain if the troops that Huger saw were going to stay at Fort Monroe or were destined to join the Union forces at New Bern, North Carolina. Just to be on the

Federal troops at Hampton, Virginia. The once beautiful town was destroyed by Confederates earlier in the war.

safe side, Johnston was directed to send 10,000 of his men to Richmond and hold the rest ready to march.

The intentions of the Union troops gathering at Fort Monroe were not at all clear when they first arrived. Initially the Yankee force advanced no farther than Hampton and so posed no threat to Magruder's position at Yorktown, about 14 miles to the west. Except for a few scouting parties, the Union forces remained quiet until 27 March, when they conducted a two-pronged reconnaissance in force towards Magruder's lines. The northern column, consisting of Heintzelman's corps, marched out along the Yorktown Road to Big Bethel and advanced its skirmishers as far as Howard's Bridge, five miles from Yorktown. Smith's division, which formed the southern column, advanced on the James River Road as far as Young's Mill, five miles east of the Confederate posts along the Warwick River. The two columns promptly returned to their camps after determining that there were no Confederate forces east of Yorktown. They also achieved their secondary mission, which was to scout the land between Hampton and Yorktown. The Yankees had no current maps of the area and were relying on a faded British map from the Revolutionary War siege at Yorktown in 1781!

After the reconnaissance, General Heintzelman, the senior Union commander until McClellan arrived, calculated Magruder's strength to be 15,000 to 20,000 men. In reality, the Confederates had only about 11,000 troops, of whom 6,000 were stationed in a portion of the old Revolutionary War lines at Yorktown and the other 5,000 were covering the 10 mile line from Yorktown south to the mouth of the Warwick River. Magruder was becoming gravely concerned about the growing enemy strength in his front, but General Lee in Richmond urged him to remain vigilant, since the Yankees in front of Yorktown could possibly be a feint in favor of an enemy movement against Norfolk.

When McClellan arrived at Fort Monroe on 2 April, he found about 60,000 of his troops there and ready for action, with many more en route. His initial plans had been to march quickly up the Peninsula towards Richmond, supported by navy fire power on the York River to the right and the James River to the left. The navy, he soon discovered, was unable to cooperate in the movement. The *Monitor* and other large warships were needed to keep the *Virginia* in check at Norfolk, and the remaining lighter vessels were not powerful enough to reduce the Confederate river batteries at Yorktown and Gloucester Point, opposite Yorktown, which together effectively closed the York River. This situation meant that McClellan would have to rely totally on his own troops to drive Magruder out of his Yorktown lines.

After surveying the situation and consulting with Heintzelman and his other officers, McClellan decided on 3 April to make an advance on Yorktown the next day. He was confident that he could take the enemy position at once, but if it proved to be stronger than expected, he would bring down more troops from Alexandria and place them on the north side of the York River. They could be used to seize Gloucester Point, so opening the York to the navy's boats, which would be able to turn Magruder's position at Yorktown and force him to retire.

McClellan's plan for his 4 April advance called for his command to march in three columns. Heintzelman was to take his *III Corps* and march on the direct road to Yorktown in order to distract Magruder while Keyes led his *IV Corps* across the Warwick River south of Yorktown. Keyes' objective would be to occupy Halfway House, five miles west of Yorktown, a move that would cut off Magruder's retreat route to Richmond. Sumner's *II Corps* would march as far as Big Bethel and remain there in reserve, ready to join in an attack on Magruder if the Confederates chose to fight rather than surrender.

McClellan's movement got off in good form early on 4 April. The roads were soon packed with troops, wagons, horses and ambulances as the army snaked its way across the flat and partially forested country towards Yorktown. The very size of the column slowed its pace, since this was the first time many of the troops had marched to action, and almost everyone brought along too much baggage and personal gear. Nevertheless, the march proceeded well and the two advance columns covered almost 12 miles during the day, though they still did not make contact with the enemy.

McClellan's plan began to go awry on 5 April, the second day of his advance. A heavy rain fell on the night of 4/5 April, and soon the roads were turned to mud and every stream became a marsh or torrent. The troops' rate of advance slowed to a crawl, and the roads were soon so mucky that the artillery and ammunition wagons could not be brought up. The worst news of the day came soon after dawn, when Keyes reported that he had come upon a "large force" of the enemy at Lee's Mill on the Warwick River, located about five miles south of Yorktown. Keyes thought that he would be in for a heavy fight, and took until noon to deploy men carefully in the muddy fields. He moved forward and engaged the enemy as best he could but could not determine their strength or the full extent of their prepared lines. Towards evening he reported to McClellan that he would not be able to reach his

UNION APPROACH TO RICHMOND, MAY 1862

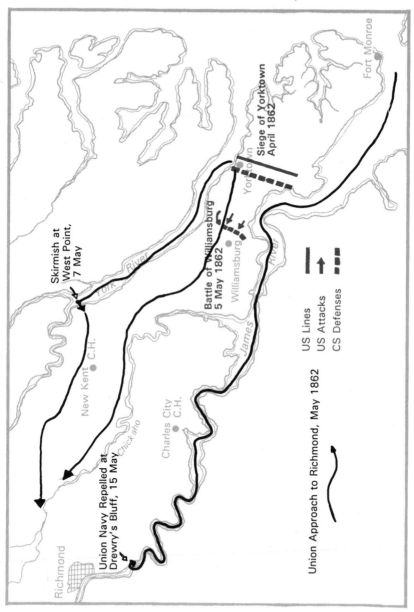

Fort Monroe

Siege of Yorktown
April 1862

Yorktown

Skirmish at
West Point,
7 May

Battle of Williamsburg
5 May 1862

Williamsburg

York River

James River

US Lines
US Attacks
CS Defenses

New Kent
C.H.

Charles City
C.H.

Chickaho

Union Navy Repelled at
Drewry's Bluff, 15 May

Union Approach to Richmond, May 1862

Richmond

goal at the Halfway House, still six miles distant, and would need help from Sumner's reserve troops just to get past Lee's Mill. He added that enemy troops were reported to be filing into position behind the Warwick River south of the mill, which meant that there would be no hope of turning the enemy's works.

McClellan was not at all pleased to hear about Keyes' lack of progress. He had gone forward with Heintzelman's troops, who had also been slowed down by the cold rain. As they approached Yorktown, the column was shelled by enemy artillery and had to stop while their cannons were laboriously brought forward through the mud and positioned to make reply. On the next day, the 6th, it became clear that the Yorktown lines could not be flanked. McClellan and his chief engineer, Brigadier General Barnard, inspected the enemy lines and found them to be too strong to take by assault. Barnard later wrote in his official report, "They are far more extensive than may be supposed from the mention of them I make, and every kind of obstruction which the country affords, such as abatis, marsh, inundation, etc., was skillfully used. The line is certainly one of the most extensive known to modern times. The country on both sides of the Warwick from near Yorktown down is a dense forest with few clearings. It was swampy and the roads impassable during the heavy rains we have constantly had except where our labors had corduroyed them."

Faced with what he judged to be a formidable defense manned by a force judged to number 30,000 men, McClellan made one of the most critical decisions of the war. Even though time was of the essence in order to reach Richmond before Johnston could be bought down from Fredericksburg, McClellan directed that his troops stop and make siege lines while he brought up his heavy guns and siege equipment. It took him three days to establish a new supply base at Cheeseman's Creek, located on the York River five miles from Yorktown. He then took his time constructing earthworks and

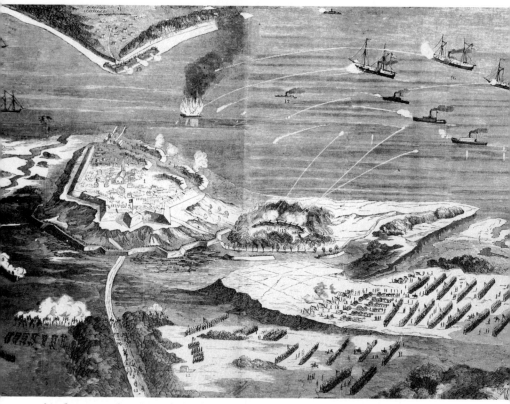

Yorktown, the site of the famous Revolutionary War battle where the U.S. won its independence, was also host to the Civil War. McClellan delayed his advance up the Peninsula several weeks to give siege to Confederate forces entrenched there.

bringing up the siege guns that, he was certain, would guarantee him victory. He had previously planned to use McDowell's troops to outflank any enemy forces that blocked his path, but on 5 April he received the disconcerting news that Lincoln would not release McDowell's command and was retaining it as a covering force for Washington because McClellan had failed to leave behind as many troops as he had pledged. This news reenforced McClellan's decision to begin a siege at Yorktown.

Magruder was utterly amazed that the Yankee army, which outnumbered his command at least four-to-one, did not launch an assault against his thin lines. A less confident commander might well have evacuated Yorktown rather than run the risk of being captured or cut off from Richmond. Magruder, however, decided to stay and bluff McClellan, and in so doing he performed a great service to the Confederacy. He ordered his troops to be aggressive, and shifted them around frequently in order to give the impression that he was receiving reinforcements and had more men than he actually did. As already stated, he held slightly over half of his 11,000 men in the works at Yorktown, with the remainder spread out along the Warwick River. The latter line was far from continuous; had he stretched out his command the men would have formed a weak skirmish line with one man posted approximately every 10 feet. Magruder instead chose to concentrate his available men and guns at a few key points such as Lee's Mill that were most exposed to enemy attack. The strategy worked well, and deterred the Yankees from trying to cross the rain swollen Warwick River, which was not defended for its entire length as McClellan thought.

Magruder's successful bravado at Yorktown brought critical time for Johnston to bring his army south from Fredericksburg. Johnston arrived ahead of his troops for an inspection of the situation on 12 April, and was not at all pleased with what he saw. Magruder's lines were adequate enough to delay McClellan, he thought, but they were vulnerable to enemy heavy guns. In addition, there was a serious weak point in the position between the Yorktown fortifications and the ponds that Magruder created at the head of the Warwick River. The greatest weakness of the line was that it could be easily turned by a naval movement up either the James and or the York River. In that case, all the troops in the Yorktown lines would be in danger of being captured or destroyed.

Johnston hurried to Richmond on the morning of 14 April and strongly urged the evacuation of Magruder's force as well as Huger's command at Norfolk. It would be much better, he argued, to bring up reinforcements from Georgia and the Carolinas in order to form a large army at Richmond that would be capable of defeating McClellan in the field once the Yankees made their way up the Peninsula away from their supply base. The meeting developed into a day long conference when Davis invited Secretary of War Randolph and Generals Lee, G. W. Smith and Longstreet to come and give their opinions. Lee and Randolph did not wish to abandon Yorktown and Norfolk, while Smith argued for an offensive against Washington since McClellan was bogged down before Yorktown. Longstreet, offended at being interrupted by Davis, said little. Since consensus could not be reached, the final decision was up to Davis. The president opted to try to hold Norfolk and Yorktown as long as possible. He may have been swayed by the need for time to reorganize Johnston's army as the 12 months' volunteers reenlisted and the new conscription law took effect.

Johnston dutifully obeyed orders and soon had most of his command transferred to the Yorktown front. This gave him a total force of about 53,000 men to face McClellan's growing command that would soon be twice the size of the Confederate army. Though Johnston was not eager to be fighting on the Yorktown line, he did succeed at gaining permission from President Davis to have Magruder's troops and the force at Norfolk placed under his command. This, at least, would give the Confederates a unified command for the campaign.

Johnston set his men to work completing and strengthening the works that Magruder had started. There was also a pressing need to cut roads through the pine woods. Soon the troops were so exhausted from their manual labor that slaves had to be pressed into duty; as early as 11 April, Magruder had ordered that each local land owner had to supply one man equipped with an axe or spade for army service. The newly constructed trenches quickly filled with water from the heavy rains that made life uncomfortable for the men of both armies. There were regular exchanges of artillery fire all along the Yorktown lines, and accurate shots from sharp-shooters (primarily Colonel Hiram Berdan's green clad United States Sharpshooters and volunteers from Hood's Texas Brigade) made life dangerous for the careless. Almost all of the fighting, though, was carried on at long distance, and more blood may have been lost to mosquitoes than to enemy fire. One of the few direct clashes occurred on 16 April when part of the *Vermont Brigade* was sent on a reconnaissance across a pond near Lee's Mill. The Vermonters managed to surprise and rout the 15th North Carolina but were in turn driven back by Cobb's brigade; some of the Yankees drowned while recrossing the pond, and casualties amounted to about 75 men on each side. After this affair, the troops on both sides became increasingly apprehensive of enemy forays, especially after dark. Many of the men became exhausted from being regularly called to form battle lines before dawn to meet enemy assaults that never came. Under these conditions, it is no wonder that numerous soldiers on both sides fell ill with camp fevers and other maladies.

Johnston was thankful that McClellan did not conduct an attack, because his command was in disarray for most of April. Many of his 12 months' enlistees were transferring to other units or demanding their reenlistment furloughs, while others, tired of life in the army, chose to let their enlistments expire so they could go home. The Confederate camps were buzzing with complaints about the draft instituted on 16 April, and almost every regiment was preparing to elect new officers. One Tennessee private noted that "candidates became more plentiful than voters." Major General D. H. Hill complained that all the elections and the rearrangement of his regiments made it so that "I scarcely know my officers by name." General Johnston wrote Lee that "The troops in addition to the lax discipline of volunteers, are particularly discontented at the conscription act and demoralized by their recent elections."

The Yankees were also busy constructing fortifications for

Union Mortar Battery No. 4 at Yorktown. McClellan hoped that bringing up his heavy guns would allow him to blast the Confederates out of their strong positions. His enemies retreated before "Young Napoleon" could test his plan.

Troops of the Vermont Brigade skirmish with Confederates near Yorktown on 16 April.

THE PENINSULA CAMPAIGN

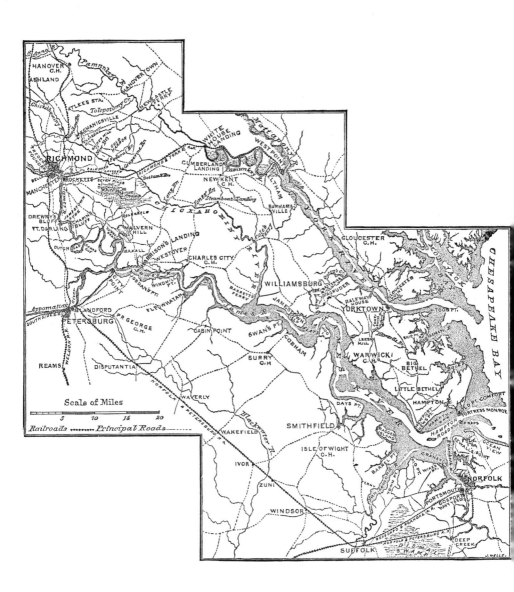

the rest of April. For the first 10 days after he reached York-town, McClellan laid out lines and had his men construct roads, bridges and earthworks. They were given no rest, and were constantly at work when not on picket duty or sleeping. One soldier in the *13th Massachusetts* wrote of his travail: "A majority of the regiment, and sometimes the whole of it, were daily detailed for fatigue duty and reported with arms and equipment at corps headquarters, where every man was fur-nished with an ax or a spade...Bridges and roads were con-structed in the ravines for the passage of cannon and ammunition; and ditches, revetments, and parapets were built in the advance."

Almost all the Union works were constructed opposite the Confederate lines at Yorktown, where the ground was much more open and offered better fields of fire. When the first parallel of entrenchments was completed about one-half mile from the enemy lines, additional parallels were made in order to get closer to the Confederate works. Most of the digging had to be started at night, since enemy fire made it too dan-gerous to be seen in the daylight; the small initial trenches started at night were then expanded and deepened in the daytime.

McClellan was under great pressure from Secretary Stan-ton and other officials to get "on to Richmond," but he would not be rushed in his preparations. His plan was to mount over 100 heavy guns, including 13-inch mortars and 200-pound Parrott rifles, that would blast the enemy works and prepare the way for an infantry assault at the weak spot in the Con-federate lines between Lee's Mill and Yorktown. By 1 May, 12 of his 14 batteries were in position, and some of the big guns in Battery Number One, located next to the York River, began banging away. Their discharges made the earth shudder, but caused few casualties. Their powerful shells went screaming beyond the Confederate works and killed some wild dogs that had been running loose in Yorktown all winter.

McClellan scheduled his grand assault for 4 May. John-

One of the impressive array of guns that McClellan gathered at Yorktown, a 200-pound Parrot Rifle.

ston had no intention of remaining to receive it whenever it would come. By the end of April all indications were that McClellan's preparations were nearing completion and the enemy might attack any day. Johnston had no heavy artillery to answer McClellan's siege guns, and he was becoming increasingly concerned that a Federal naval movement up the York River might cut him off from Richmond. After lengthy correspondence with Davis and Lee, Johnston finally obtained permission to withdraw from his Yorktown lines.

Johnston ordered the withdrawal to begin on 2 May, but faulty staff work and a rainstorm delayed the movement until the night of 3 May. Johnston made careful arrangements for the march, and sent two divisions (Longstreet's and Magruder's) along the James River Road while his other two divisions (Smith's and Hill's) travelled on a more northerly route. In order to cover the movement, several artillery detachments stayed behind to maintain a covering fire and General Stuart sent dismounted cavalrymen to man the picket lines. These troops held their positions until about 0300, when they hastily withdrew. Johnston was gravely criticized for leaving 56 cannons behind in his works, though it must be admitted that he could not have withdrawn all his guns without alerting the enemy to his intentions.

Except for the loss of the cannons, Johnston's withdrawal came off smoothly. The Yankees were more relieved than concerned when the Confederate guns quit firing at 0300 on 4 May. They did not notice that anything was amiss until sunrise, when their newly posted pickets did not draw enemy fire as usual. Soon the cry swept back from the front lines that the enemy had fled. Its effect was electric: "Loud cheers resounded along the line, from the York River to Warwick Creek, when the result was officially announced; and the bands, which had been dumb so long, again enlivened the soldiers." Soon troops were marching gleefully into Yorktown, eager to explore the town and the abandoned Confederate works. Their enthusiasm was dampened when several fell victim to primitive land mines called "torpedoes" that the Confederates had left behind (see sidebar).

Federal troops occupy the vacated Yorktown fortifications. Johnston abandoned his position there to avoid McClellan's assault which was finally ready to begin in early May.

Land Mines

Perhaps the first use of land mines in modern warfare occurred at Yorktown during the Peninsula Campaign. Confederate Brigadier General Gabriel J. Rains had some of his men bury 8-and 10-inch Columbiad artillery shells a few inches in the ground to help guard his works. The shells (called "torpedoes" in this use) were set with fulminate or artillery friction primers so that they would explode when stepped on; the Confederates may also have used lanyards to explode them, but there is no evidence that they employed trip wires. It is not known how many of the "torpedoes" caused casualties during combat. They gained great notoriety after the Confederates retreated from Yorktown, when a small number of unsuspecting Union soldiers stepped on some and were killed or had their legs blown off. The psychological effect of the mines was much greater than the actual damage they did, as the devices forced the Union troops to move through the deserted Confederate works with extra caution. Union artillery chief W.F. Barry claimed that the "torpedoes" were not placed just in front of the defenses, but also "on common roads, at springs of water, in the shade of trees, at the foot of telephone poles, and lastly, quite within the defenses of the place—in the very streets." General McClellan in his *Memoirs* says that he used Confederate prisoners to lo-

cate and remove the "torpedoes"; this action may have been in response to a report that the Confederates had forced Union sympathizers to bury these primitive land mines in the first place.

The employment of "torpedoes" at wells and on common roadways was thought to be "unsporting" by both Union and Confederate officers. Major General James Longstreet, Rains' wing commander, directed during the retreat from Williamsburg that Rains plant no more shells or "torpedoes" "as he does not recognize it as a proper or effective method of war." When Rains and his division commander, Major General D.H. Hill, objected that "torpedoes" were legitimate for use in retreat and for the defense of works, Confederate Secretary of War George W. Randolph issued a directive stating that "It is not admissible in civilized warfare to take life with no other object than the destruction of life...It is admissible to plant shells in a parapet to repel an assault, or in a wood to check pursuit, because the object is to save the work in one case and the army in the other."

It turns out that the whole controversy may have been very much overblown. Because of the brouhaha in the newspapers, Confederate army commander General Joe Johnston requested Hill to get the truth of the matter from Rains. Rains admitted to implanting "torpedoes" in front of his works at Yorktown for defensive reasons. The only "torpedoes" he set in roadways were four abandoned artillery shells he hastily buried in the road some six miles short of Williamsburg when he was commanding the army's rear guard during the retreat from Yorktown. These, he said, "were hastily prepared by my efforts, and put in the road near a tree felled across, mainly to have a moral effect in checking the advance of the enemy." In this he certainly succeeded. Other reported instances of "torpedoes" exploding on roads or in the town may have been caused by shells that had fired and landed unexploded, and then went off when disturbed later.

CHAPTER V

Williamsburg

*I*n spite of all his elaborate arrangements for the siege of Yorktown, McClellan had no contingency plans prepared for a pursuit should the enemy suddenly retreat as Johnston did on the night of 3/4 May. As soon as he learned of Johnston's withdrawal, he sent Brigadier General George Stoneman in pursuit with four cavalry regiments and four batteries of horse artillery. Stoneman was supported by Keyes' *IV Corps*, which took the James River Road, and Heintzelman's *III Corps*, which followed the more northerly route west from Williamsburg. McClellan ordered the rest of his army to wait in readiness to march, and then went to the Yorktown wharves to make arrangements to send Franklin's division up the York River on transports.

Stoneman's cavalry caught up with Johnston's rear guard, formed by a portion of Stuart's cavalry, near the Halfway House, located about six miles west of Yorktown. Stuart conducted a delaying action for about two miles before appealing to Johnston for help. Johnston at the time was at Williamsburg, which the last of the Confederate infantry had reached by noon. Their march had become a slow one, since only one highway extended west from Williamsburg, so Johnston had allowed his rear divisions to rest while they waited for the troops ahead of them to clear the road. When he received Stuart's request for assistance, Johnston moved two infantry brigades into Fort Magruder, an earthen redoubt that had been constructed the previous month astride the main Yorktown Road about a mile east of Williamsburg. The fort was several hundred yards long with ramparts about six feet high, and was supported by smaller redoubts on each flank.

The Confederate infantry had not occupied Fort Magruder long before Stoneman's cavalry came up at mid-afternoon. Stoneman made a few feeble attacks on the Confederate line, and withdrew to await his supporting infantry, which soon came up. Towards evening General Sumner, as senior officer on the field, took command of the situation and ordered an assault to be made by Smith's division. However, it soon grew dark and Smith's men lost their way in the thick underbrush, so the attack was canceled.

After darkness fell, Johnston relieved the two brigades holding Fort Magruder and sent them on their way towards Richmond. He replaced them with two fresh brigades from Longstreet's Division, R.H. Anderson's and Pryor's, which were intended to serve as a rear guard until the army cleared Williamsburg. Brigadier General R.H. Anderson as senior officer took charge of the post and occupied Fort Magruder along with 6 of its 12 supporting redoubts. It was not easy for the Confederate troops to find their posts, as Private Jesse Reid wrote: "It was a very dark night, cloudy and drizzling rain. We nearly ran into the enemy's lines before we knew it. Three men were put at each post, with orders to stay awake all night, and for one of us to crawl out towards the enemy's lines and find out, if possible, their position. I crawled out to a fence post one hundred yards...I could distinctly hear them talking but could see nothing on account of the darkness."

The rain mentioned by Private Reid severely hindered McClellan's pursuit plans. The roads from Yorktown to Williamsburg were turned to quagmires full of troops in one giant traffic jam. As a result, no one made much progress that night. When dawn came on the 5th, Brigadier General Joseph Hooker seemed to be the only officer interested in pushing the Confederates. He felt that all the other Union generals were too timid, so on his own initiative he had his men on the

Joseph Hooker. A divisional commander in the III Corps *during the Peninsula campaign, Hooker would rise to command the* Army of the Potomac *almost a year later.*

march towards Williamsburg at dawn. It was not long before the head of his column emerged from a woods to find itself face to face with the Confederate rear guard at Fort Magruder. Hooker was in no mood to avoid a fight, and at once sent his men headlong into action without even reconnoitering the ground first. His reasons for doing so are not clear today; he may have been overeager to fight, or he may have attacked the enemy deliberately in order to bring on the general engagement he thought his superiors were reluctant to attempt.

Hooker's attack gave the tired Confederate defenders a hard time. Private Reid continues: "Just at daylight the enemy commenced snapping caps on their guns—to dry their tubes, I suppose. I will admit that I never felt so nervous in my life...A little after daylight they appeared in large numbers and attacked...We held our ground as long as possible, giving them as good as they sent until about seven o'clock, when they came in such overwhelming numbers as to force us back to our main lines, a distance of about six hundred yards."

Hooker moved his three brigades forward gradually towards the redoubts on the right of Fort Magruder. To his dismay, no additional troops came to his aid except his own divisional artillery, which experienced a great deal of difficulty forming up opposite Fort Magruder. By now Confederate General James Longstreet, whose troops were still in Williamsburg, was aware of the fighting. About 0800 he sent two brigades under Brigadier Generals Wilcox and A. P. Hill to assist Anderson, and an hour later he committed the rest of his division, consisting of Pickett's and Colston's brigades. These fresh troops came up on Anderson's right and soon gave Hooker's men a hard time: "About eleven o'clock we saw emerging from the little ravine to the left of the fort a swarm of Confederates, who opened fire on us with a terrible and deadly fire. Then they charged upon us with their peculiar yell. We took all the advantage possible of the stumps and trees as we were pushed back, until we reached the edge of the wood again, where we halted and fired upon the enemy from behind all the cover the situation offered."

Longstreet's fresh brigades slowly overwhelmed Hooker's weary division and in the process captured one of Hooker's batteries. Hooker was disheartened to see his units begin to collapse, especially since there were two fresh divisions of Sumner's corps not far to his right. Sumner, however, was stubbornly refusing to weaken his position as he made preparations to attack the Confederate left. The only general apparently interested in helping Hooker was his corps commander, Samuel Heintzelman. Heintzelman had been with Sumner most of the morning, and about 1300 came over to see how Hooker was doing. He was greatly discouraged by the condition of Hooker's men and immediately tried to cheer them up. He assembled several regimental bands and ordered "Play! Play! It's all you're good for. Play! Damn it! Play some marching tune! Play 'Yankee Doodle' or any doodle you can think of, only play something."

Hooker's hard pressed division had to wait another two hours for help to arrive. Aid at last came not from Sumner's command, but from Heintzelman's other division, led by Brigadier General Phil Kearny, which had been delayed for hours by the mud and wagons on the Hampton Road. By that hour, Longstreet's attack had begun to run out of steam, and additional Union reinforcements were arriving to tilt the battle in favor of the Federal cause. Even so, the fighting on the left did not die down until sunset.

The battle on the Union right was much slower to develop than the action on Hooker's front. As already mentioned, Major General Edwin Sumner was reluctant to begin his attack or even give support to Hooker until all his troops were up. The only serious offensive action he actually took during the day came late in the morning when he sent Brigadier General Winfield Hancock with a makeshift brigade to capture an unoccupied redoubt on the far left of the Confederate line. Hancock easily did so, and was amazed to find that the enemy was unaware that he was perched on their flank. He quickly sent to his division commander, W. F. Smith, for reinforcements, and dug in to await their arrival.

As the day wore on, Hancock's position became more and more precarious when Confederate troops started gathering on his front. He sent several messengers to his superiors,

Generals Smith and Sumner, to plead for reinforcements, since he was two miles in front of Smith's line and could not hold on by himself indefinitely. Sumner stubbornly refused to send aid because he was still awaiting reinforcements, and at length gruffly ordered another of Hancock's messengers to tell the general to pull back.

Hancock refused to follow Sumner's orders. He realized that he was in an advantageous position to flank the enemy's line, and on his own initiative ordered his batteries to begin shelling Fort Magruder, which was then under attack by Couch's newly arrived division. Hancock's guns caught the attention of Confederate Brigadier General Jubal Early, whose troops were still in Williamsburg. Early was eager for action, and secured permission from his division commander, D. H. Hill, to make an attack on Hancock's guns.

Early took off directly for Hancock's cannons. Because it was so late in the day (after 1700), the Confederate general did not take time to reconnoiter first. His haste brought disastrous results. He had to pass through a large woods in order to get at Hancock. The woods slowed down his center two regiments while the units on each flank, the 24th Virginia and the 5th North Carolina, rushed impetuously ahead. The two regiments emerged from the woods in clear view of the enemy and could not have been in a worse position—neither had any support, and their lines were at an awkward angle that put them under a terrible enfilading fire from Hancock's entire brigade. Nevertheless, the two units pressed on, suffering horrendous casualties. General Early was wounded in the shoulder and the 24th Virginia lost 190 men, about half its strength. General Hill witnessed the slaughter of 5th North Carolina, a dreadful scene that he never forgot: "The regiment was shot down like beeves, the Yankees cheering and laughing as they fired at the poor fellows." The unfortunate regiment lost its battle flag and over half of its men.

Early's attack was a tragic waste of manpower, as it had no effect on the outcome of the battle. McClellan finally arrived on the battlefield just as Early was being repulsed, and decided that it was too late in the day to push the battle further. He had been inexplicably absent from the battle all day, leaving control of the battle to Sumner's unwilling hands. When he finally arrived, though, he did not hesitate to take partial credit for Hancock's victory. Indeed, he called the entire battle a glorious Union success, even though his troops suffered more casualties than the Confederates. After all, the Federal soldiers forced the enemy to abandon the battlefield, and McClellan's men easily occupied Williamsburg the next day. Johnston, on the other hand, also claimed the victory for his side. He had been on the field most of the day, and saw his troops victorious all down the line except for Early's unfortunate and ill-advised attack. His rear guard had done its job well, and was withdrawn during the night to join the rest of the army on its way towards Richmond.

The battle of Williamsburg is perhaps best viewed as a draw. It was by far the largest battle of the war in the East up to that point, and was clearly remembered by all the troops on both sides who saw their first combat there. Today the battle is not well known because it was so overshadowed by the later huge engagements of the campaign and the war. Final figures show that there were 40,768 Federals on the field, of whom only 9,000 were engaged. They suffered 2,239 casualties (456 killed, 1,410 wounded, and 373 missing; 1,600 of the casualties were from Hooker's division alone). The Confederates had 31,823 men on the field, about half of whom were actively engaged. Their losses totaled 1,603 men.

CHAPTER VI

On to Richmond

Confederate General Joe Johnston continued marching his weary army on the road to Richmond after fighting the rear guard action at Williamsburg on 5 May 1862. He was grieved at having to leave his wounded behind on the battlefield, but he had no choice. There was no time to recover them as more Yankee troops came up, ready to renew the battle on the 6th, and he did not have enough transport to carry them anyway. He pulled his last troops, one of D.H. Hill's brigades, out of Williamsburg at about 2300 on the 5th, and ordered it to follow the rest of the army on the road to Barhamsville, 18 miles to the northwest. The only aid he could give his wounded left at Williamsburg was to send back some surgeons under a flag of truce on the 6th. The Confederate dead had to be left to be buried by enemy hands in shallow graves.

Johnston's infantry and artillery experienced a great deal of difficulty marching northwest out of Williamsburg on the only available road, which was a mucky morass from recent rains and from overuse. The head of the column, composed of Smith's and Magruder's divisions, reached Barhamsville on the afternoon of the 6th. Johnston sent Magruder on towards Richmond and directed Smith to wait and cover the arrival of Hill's and Longstreet's divisions, which had done the fighting at Williamsburg. He also directed Smith to post pickets on the York River east of Barhamsville with instructions to be on the alert for any Union surprise attack from the river.

Johnston was wise to watch his flank along the York River.

After the battle at Williamsburg was ended, McClellan decided that the roads were too poor and his men on the field were too tired and disorganized to mount an effective pursuit of Johnston's rear guard. The divisions at Williamsburg needed to be resupplied, and their wagons were still stuck in the mud on the roads from Yorktown. In addition, the wounded needed care, and the dead of both sides needed burial. For these reasons, he sent only a token force to pursue Johnston. The rest of the troops were given three days' rest at Williamsburg, time they used to visit the town and tour the battlefield. They did not hesitate to pick up souvenirs and gawk at the dead laid out for burial. It would not be long before such dreadful sights would be commonplace.

McClellan did not send his troops in direct pursuit of Johnston's army after Williamsburg because he had another plan in mind—to cut off Johnston's retreat by sending a task force up the York River on naval transports. Ever since the last days of the siege at Yorktown, he had been holding Franklin's newly arrived division in readiness for just such a move. As soon as Yorktown was captured, McClellan rushed to the town's docks in order to make arrangements to gather his transports and embark Franklin's men. Poor docking facilities and bad weather combined to thwart his efforts for two days. The greatest difficulty was encountered trying to load the artillery batteries and their horses. In addition, several days' supply of provisions and forage also had to be loaded on the boats. McClellan remained in Yorktown most of 5 May to make arrangements for the expedition, and thus missed almost all of the battle of Williamsburg. Despite all his efforts, he could not gather enough vessels to carry more than one division of troops. This meant that Franklin would be on his own during the foray and would have only naval warships for support.

The small flotilla carrying Franklin's men finally got under way from Yorktown on the morning of 6 May. The troops were carried on an odd collection of barges, schooners, steamers, iron-clads and some canal boats that were fastened together and decked over in order to serve as floating wharves, all shepherded by naval warships. The convoy reached its goal at West Point, 20 miles upriver from Yorktown, at mid-afternoon, and began preparations to disembark at nearby Eltham's Landing, located on the opposite (south) shore of the mouth of the Pamunkey River. Had it arrived 24 hours earlier, the amphibious force might have seized Barhamsville or New Kent Court House and caused much discomfort to Johnston's withdrawal. As it was, Franklin's men came under Confederate artillery fire as soon as they tried to effect a landing. Smith's Confederate outposts were aware of their coming and had a warm reception prepared.

Franklin feverishly set his men to work establishing a defensive line as soon as they landed. The whole force was ashore by dawn and he set about realigning his position in the daylight. Franklin had no maps of the area and also had no idea how many troops were opposing him, so he sat still to await whatever reinforcements McClellan could send him by water or by land. His lack of aggressiveness was all too clear in the following note he sent to McClellan that day: "I congratulate myself that we have maintained our position."

Though Johnston was not aware of the size, scope, and intent of Franklin's force, he dealt with the situation quite effectively. He called Magruder's division back to Barhamsville to support Smith, and directed Smith to move his command forward to neutralize Franklin. Longstreet's and Hill's divisions were held in readiness to support Smith if needed. Smith, though, was not eager to attack the enemy because he feared the fire power of the Yankee boats in the river. Instead, he decided to try to find a sheltered position where he could position some artillery to shell the enemy camps and transports and so delay them long enough to enable the rest of the Confederate army to get a good head start on the road to Richmond.

Smith sent Brigadier General W.H.C. Whiting with Hampton's and Hood's brigades to deal with Franklin. Whiting readily pushed the Federal skirmishers aside and then skillfully shoved the enemy line back over a mile through the woods to the edge of the river. When Franklin's command sought shelter under a high bluff near the river, Whiting found he could not reach them with his cannons, nor were the Federal transports within range. Nevertheless, he and his two brigadiers won commendation for their efforts as they held Franklin in check, allowing the rest of their army time to retire to the west.

Johnston decided to form a temporary line approximately 15 miles east of Richmond and there await McClellan's advance. Longstreet and Hill were directed to march to the Long Bridge over the Chickahominy River, while Smith and Magruder proceeded along the New Kent Road from Barhamsville to Baltimore Cross Roads, located near the Richmond and York River Railroad about five miles north of Long Bridge. Johnston was quite pleased with the new position, since it was easily supplied by the railroad and his flanks were secure, since neither the Pamunkey River on his left nor the Chickahominy on his right were navigable by the larger Union warships. The Confederate troops remained on this line for five days of much needed rest.

McClellan was in no hurry to pursue Johnston, and began a leisurely advance from Williamsburg that was often slowed by rain and mud. His advance guard, consisting of Stoneman's cavalry command reinforced by two infantry regiments, did not reach Franklin's front until late on 8 May, a full day after the Confederates had evacuated the area. He then pushed on through New Kent Court House and on the 11th occupied White House, a Lee family estate near the Richmond and York River Railroad bridge over the Pamunkey River. McClellan began moving his infantry forward on the 8th, after they had been resupplied at Williamsburg. His march was slow and deliberate because of all his supply trains and the bad roads; at one stretch he covered only five miles in

General McClellan's Army of the Potomac *slowly makes its way through the swamps and forests of the Peninsula on its way to the Confederate capital at Richmond. McClellan moved so slowly that one of his generals called him the "Virginia Creeper."*

forty-eight hours. At length, the Union divisions began arriving at White House on the 15th. McClellan had determined to use White House as his base for the next stage of his drive on Richmond, and he set up his headquarters there on 16 May.

While McClellan's troops were inching their way towards Richmond, everyone's attention turned to the south side of the James River. Johnston's evacuation of Yorktown on 3 May had isolated Major General Benjamin Huger's division-sized command at Norfolk and meant that he, too, had to withdraw to the west before being isolated and captured. President Davis had been most reluctant to give up Norfolk, since it was the site of the important Gosport Navy Yard, home base to the ironclad warship *Virginia*. To be certain, the *Virginia* had not taken the offensive since its destructive spree on 8 March, due to the timely arrival of the Union *Monitor*. It nevertheless remained a great source of concern to the Yankee fleet, and was still useful for restraining the enemy from withdrawing their warships for a dash up the James River towards Richmond. Prospects for the survival of the *Virginia* did not look good if Norfolk had to be abandoned. The ironclad did not have the stamina to break through its Union guards and head south towards North Carolina, and its draught was too great to enable it to escape up the James. This left the Confederates no choice but to blow up the ship to keep it from falling into enemy hands after they evacuated Norfolk on 9 May. Huger then began marching his command towards Petersburg, as ordered by General Lee.

The news that the Confederates had evacuated Norfolk came as very cheerful news to President Lincoln and Secretary of War Stanton, who had sailed to Fort Monroe following the capture of Yorktown in order to urge the capture of the *Virginia*'s base. Curiously, the two officials spent all their time with Commodore Goldsborough and General John E. Wool, the commander at Fort Monroe, and did not attempt to see McClellan before returning to Washington on 11 May. They no doubt figured that McClellan was too busy with his army at the front after the battle of Williamsburg, which was doubtless true.

McClellan was also delighted when he heard of the destruction of the *Virginia*, because he understood that the James River was now open as a Federal highway to Richmond. On 15 May he sent a squadron of warship, including the *Monitor*, up the James to threaten and possibly capture the Confederate capital. The Confederates had long dreaded such an attack, and had worked hard to erect a fort at Drewry's Bluff, located on the west bank of the James some seven miles south of Richmond. The river narrowed to about a mile there as it made a 90 degree bend to the north, and the Confederates used pilings and large boulders to try to narrow its channel. At midday on 15 May the Union flotilla arrived and began a noisy four hour battle. The Federals were disappointed that they could make no headway against the Confederate batteries that had the advantage of high bluffs and plunging defensive fire. They withdrew that afternoon, and Richmond was relieved to have dodged another bullet.

The fight at Drewry's Bluff underscored Johnston's concern about his ability to meet a Union infantry advance up the James. For this reason he withdrew all his infantry to the west side of the Chickahominy late on 15 May. Because the ground there proved to be too swampy, he withdrew two days later to another line only three miles from Richmond. His right flank still covered the Richmond and York River Railroad, with a watchful eye turned towards the James River, while his center and left were behind the Chickahominy as far north as Meadow Bridge and the railroad to Fredericksburg. Johnston's army was at last at the position he had wanted to occupy six weeks earlier. He told one of his aides, "The folly of sending this army down the Peninsula is only equalled by our good fortune in getting away from there." He was indeed lucky to have escaped with his army virtually intact from an enemy army almost twice his size. McClellan's deliberateness and poor decisions had cost him all the advantage he gained from his surprise amphibious movement to Fort Monroe at the start of the campaign. He had also given Johnston the time the Confederates urgently needed to reorganize their regiments and conduct their elections for new regimental officers.

McClellan was still in no hurry to push forward as the Confederates formed their new lines behind the Chickahominy at mid-month. He used two days of dry weather on 17 and 18 May to bring up supplies and finish concentrating his command at his new base at White House. He then decided that he needed to reorganize his army before beginning the final push on Richmond. He had not been pleased with the way that his three corps commanders, Sumner, Heintzelman and Keyes, had mishandled the fight at Williamsburg, and had asked Lincoln for permission to reassign them. Lincoln eventually consented, but with a hint that it did not seem to

General McClellan mounted on his steed Daniel Webster at White House. This marvelous plantation, once the property of George Washington's wife Martha Custis, was owned by Robert E. Lee's son William. White House was confiscated as McClellan's headquarters during the Peninsula campaign.

be wise to change all the army's top commanders on the eve of the coming great battle.

McClellan thought the matter over further, and decided to keep Sumner, Heintzelman and Keyes in command, but he would weaken their power by reducing the size of their commands from three divisions to two divisions each. He would then integrate the surplus divisions with newly arrived units to create two new corps, the *V* and *VI*, to be commanded by two of his friends, Fitz-John Porter and William B. Franklin. This new army structure was announced on 18 May. Couch's *II Corps* had only two divisions, Richardson's and Sedgwick's, and would retain them. Heintzelman's *III Corps* lost one division and would keep Kearny's and Hooker's. Keyes' *IV Corps* lost one division and would keep Couch's and Casey's. Porter would command the newly formed *V Corps*, consisting of his old division (formerly in Heintzelman's corps), now commanded by Brigadier General George W. Morell, and Brigadier General George Sykes' newly formed division, which consisted of two brigades of United States Regulars' infantry from the army's general reserve, along with three other regiments. Franklin would command the newly formed *VI Corps*, consisting of his division (formerly in Keyes' corps), now commanded by Brigadier General W.F. Smith, and Brigadier General Henry W. Slocum's division, recently arrived from the Department of the Rappahannock.

It should be noted that McClellan's command included no *I Corps*. This was because McClellan continued to consider Major General Irvin McDowell's command at Fredericksburg to be his *I Corps*, even though Lincoln had formed it into an independent Department of the Rappahannock on 4 April. McClellan would in fact spend the entire campaign lobbying to have McDowell join him before Richmond. The use of McDowell's force would indeed have a serious effect on the outcome of the campaign.

McClellan later claimed that he was at the critical point of the campaign on 18 May: he had the option of advancing up the railroad from West Point to Richmond, or he could have moved his line of operations to the James River and advanced upon the Confederate capital via that route. On reflection, he later claimed that could easily have formed a new base at Malvern Hill on the James. Then, "With the aid of the gunboats and water transportation I am sure I could have occupied Petersburg and placed the army in position between that place and Richmond, so that the enemy would have been obliged to abandon his capital or to come out to attack in a position of my own choosing." This argument, though, does not bear close scrutiny. On 15 May he had told the naval authorities that he did not have the troops or the interest to move against Drewry's Bluff from his camp at White House, so it is clear that a movement along the James was not on his mind in 1862.

The Federal encampment and supply base at White House, Virginia.

What McClellan really intended to do after he reached White House was to proceed directly along the line of the railroad towards Richmond. This would give him a ready made supply line to the docks at White House, and would also provide a most useful means to transport his heavy guns to the very gates of Richmond for the siege that he knew would come. It was for this reason that he had repair crews working on the Richmond and York River Railroad as early as 10 May.

McClellan resumed his deliberate advance on Richmond on 19 May, when he personally led the newly created *V* and *VI Corps* to Tunstall's Station, about five miles west of White House. Two days later his advance guard reached New Bridge on the Chickahominy, about six miles northeast of Richmond. In the next few days he moved the bulk of his army up to the Chickahominy. Franklin advanced in the center to New Bridge, while Sumner covered the ground on the left as far as the railroad bridge. Porter held the right of the line, and cleared a Confederate outpost out of Mechanicsville on the 24th. Meanwhile, the *IV Corps* began crossing near Bottom's Bridge, one mile southeast of the railroad bridge, on the 20th. It then advanced about five miles to take up a strong position at Seven Pines, just south of Fair Oaks Station and about three miles south of New Bridge. Heintzelman's *III Corps* was crossed to the eastern side of Bottom's Bridge, but remained at least four miles behind Keyes. The railroad line from White House to the Chickahominy was fully repaired by 26 May, and McClellan was at last prepared for the next stage of his operation.

The capital of the Confederacy, Richmond, Virginia. As the Army of the Potomac drew closer to Richmond, President Davis and his military adviser Robert E. Lee pressed General Johnston to attack. The result was the indecisive Confederate foray at Gaines' Mill.

CHAPTER VII

Johnston Strikes Back

The people of Richmond were gravely concerned as McClellan's huge army approached almost to within sight of the city. Johnston had not yet put up a real fight to stop the enemy, and they were not certain that he would do so now. A case of near panic set in as everyone began to prepare for the worst. The new country's archives were packed up for immediate shipment, and the Confederacy's gold reserves were likewise packed for evacuation. Plans were made to evacuate commissary stores, and railroad officials were advised to move their cars to the south for safety. Numerous private citizens packed up their belongings and shipped them out by wagon or train. President Davis even began preparing contingency plans on how to keep the government functioning from Virginia's western mountains should Richmond be taken.

General Joe Johnston, commander of the army defending Richmond, was well aware that he was being pushed into a corner. During the third week in May, McClellan advanced to the Chickahominy River and occupied an eight mile long line from Mechanicsville to Bottom's Bridge. On 24 May the enemy advanced one corps (Keyes') to occupy Seven Pines, some three miles south of the Chickahominy and only six miles from Richmond. Reports were that this command was digging in, presumably as a base for the final stage of McClellan's drive on the capital. At the same time McClellan was extending his right flank up the Chickahominy in an effort to put more pressure on Richmond from the north. Then came the disturbing news on 27 May that Union General Irvin McDowell was marching his command of at least 30,000 men south from Fredericksburg to join McClellan.

The threat posed by McDowell's advance prodded Johnston into action. He previously had been planning to hold his lines against McClellan, though he did not relish the thought of facing for a second time all the heavy guns that the Yankees had arrayed at Yorktown. As McClellan drew slowly closer to Richmond, Johnston prepared his defenses and called up Huger's division from Petersburg to Drewry's Bluff. Even with this reinforcement, he still had only 60,000 men to face McClellan's army of well over 100,000. Despite these bad odds, President Davis and his military advisor, General Robert E. Lee, had been pressuring him to strike back at McClellan. The impending approach of McDowell, who would give the Yankees an even greater numerical advantage, compelled Johnston on 26 May to formulate a plan to strike at McClellan's right flank at Mechanicsville and drive it back before McDowell arrived.

Johnston reported to Davis that he would attack on 29 May, and called his generals together on the evening of the 28th to explain his plan. His strategy called for G.W. Smith to take three divisions (D.R. Jones', A.P. Hill's newly created mini-division, and his own unit, under Whiting) and strike at the far right of the Union line near Mechanicsville. Magruder would support the attack by crossing at New Bridge, while Longstreet and D.H. Hill confronted the Union force at Seven Pines. During the course of the conference, significant news arrived from Jeb Stuart's cavalry that McDowell had turned back in his march from Fredericksburg. This meant that there was less immediate need to attack north of the Chickahominy, and the generals debated Johnston's plan even more seriously. Smith began to express reservations because of the strength of the enemy line along Beaver Dam Creek, while Longstreet, Magruder and Stuart continued to support the attack. Johnston at length began to grow diffident, especially

General McClellan reconnoiters the ground before Richmond. By late May, the Federal general had his forces only a few miles from the enemy capital.

Confederates flee Mechanicsville in the face of an assault by Porter's V Corps infantry on 24 May.

James Longstreet, one of the greatest Confederate generals. Longstreet commanded a division throughout the Peninsula campaign

in view of Smith's attitude. He told Longstreet that he had selected the wrong officer for the work, and called off the attack. Because of the lateness of the hour, Johnston neglected to inform Davis of his decision. As a result, the president was unpleasantly surprised when he rode north out of Richmond on 29 May expecting to see a battle in progress.

Johnston had no way of knowing that Stuart's information was inaccurate. McDowell had not in fact been marching towards Richmond at all, but was actually moving towards the Shenandoah Valley to deal with "Stonewall" Jackson. The troops that Stuart had seen advance and then withdraw to Fredericksburg had merely been a cavalry scouting party!

Johnston was nonetheless relieved to be released of the threat posed by McDowell's potential approach. Longstreet, however, was anxious to take the offensive and continued to push for permission to attack Keyes' force at Seven Pines. He believed that Keyes was in an isolated position, and on the morning of 30 May sent out two armed reconnaissances to verify his suspicion. Brigadier General Robert E. Rodes advanced his brigade down the Charles City Road and found no enemy in the area; Brigadier General Samuel Garland went up the Williamsburg Road and ran into a strong skirmish line two miles west of Seven Pines. From this information and other scouting reports, Longstreet correctly determined that there was approximately one whole enemy corps at Seven Pines, with another on the south side of the Chickahominy near Bottom's Bridge. If the Confederates moved quickly, they would be able to crush one or possibly both of the Federal commands before McClellan could bring aid from the north side of the river.

Longstreet presented his plan in detail to Johnston that afternoon, and Johnston liked it. He was particularly swayed by the fact that the Union troops at Seven Pines were advanced too far from their supports at Bottom's Bridge. He was also encouraged by the fact that recent heavy rains had caused the Chickahominy to rise to a 20 year high and flood its already marshy banks. This meant that most of the bridges over the river were unstable or washed out and their approaches inundated. As a result, McClellan would experience difficulty getting reinforcements to his men at Seven Pines once the battle was started. It also meant that the Chickahominy would serve as a shield for Johnston's left wing, so that he could use 23 of his 27 brigades to strike at Keyes and Heintzelman.

Johnston's understanding of the situation was indeed correct. McClellan's engineers at that very moment were desperately trying to stabilize 11 temporary bridges they had erected over the swollen Chickahominy to replace the ones the Confederates had burned before withdrawing to Richmond. The flooding river put McClellan's army in a very awkward position and was a factor the Union commander failed to consider when he pushed Keyes forward to his exposed position at Seven Pines on 24 May. McClellan's main concern at the time had been to establish a base closer to Richmond from which he could move forward to begin shelling the city. Johnston's general lack of aggressiveness in the 10 months since Bull Run perhaps persuaded McClellan that there would be no danger of any Confederate counterattack.

Johnston's battle plan was very straightforward. D.H. Hill would open the battle by advancing directly up the Williamsburg Road to engage the enemy. Huger's division, recently arrived from Petersburg, would move up the Charles City Road on Hill's right and strike the left of the Federal line. At the same time, Longstreet would march up the Nine Mile Road on Hill's left and attack the Union right. Smith would support Longstreet, while Magruder would be ready to defend the river crossings if McClellan tried to reinforce Keyes. The only troops that Johnston did not assign an active role were A.P. Hill's, which were to remain deployed on the army's far left in order to keep McClellan's right pinned down. Longstreet was to hold tactical command of the troops engaged at Seven Pines, since the idea for the attack was his and he had handled his troops well at Williamsburg.

The Confederate divisions were on the road as ordered before dawn on 31 May. There had been a fierce storm on the afternoon of the 30th, one that felled trees and killed several soldiers with blasts of lightning, and the sky was still as overcast and soggy as it could be. The men were amazed that they were being ordered into battle under such conditions, with the roads being so miry and all the streams overflowing their banks. Little did they realize that the storm had been their greatest ally by washing out all of the Union bridges over the Chickahominy, so isolating Keyes and Heintzelman from the rest of the Union army.

Faulty staff work and incomplete orders from Johnston worked to sabotage the commander's battle plan before the Confederate troops started marching. At 2040 on 30 May Johnston sent orders to Huger to move up on D.H. Hill's right and "Be ready, if an action should begin on your left, to fall upon the enemy's left flank." Johnston failed to communicate

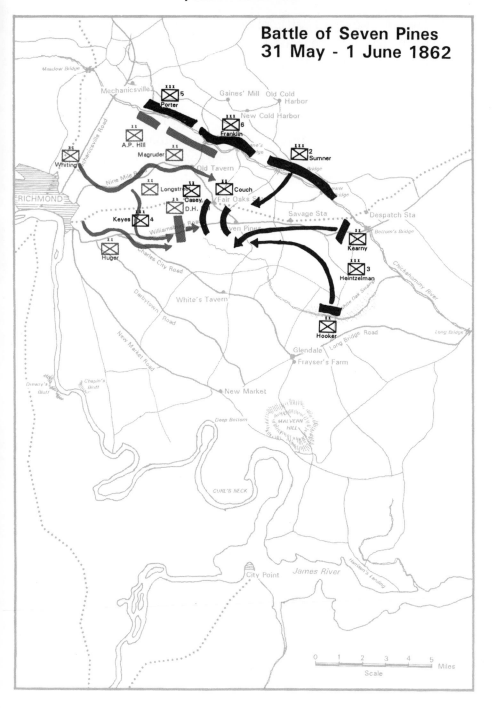

Battle of Seven Pines
31 May - 1 June 1862

to Huger his overall battle plan or the fact that Longstreet was to be in charge at the front. Likewise Johnston neglected to tell Smith of the day's battle plan. At 2115 on 30 May he wrote him that D.H. Hill would attack the enemy on his front in the morning. Smith was ordered only to bring his men to the junction of the Nine Mile and New Bridge Roads. Thus two of the four key Confederate division commanders were not clearly informed of what was to be expected of them in the battle. To make matters worse, Johnston's orders to Longstreet were given orally and may not have been fully understood.

Johnston's plan called for three Confederate columns to advance along three different roads to strike the enemy in their front. The army's approach should have been carried out smoothly but was not due to a number of problems—faulty staff work, the uncertain command structure at the front, the inexperience of all the troops from generals down to privates, and the poor weather conditions. The greatest confusion during the approach, however, was caused by none other than Major General James Longstreet, the originator of the attack plan. Longstreet's final orders had been to march out the Nine Mile Road and strike the Union right near Fair Oaks Station. For some reason Longstreet's men were slow getting started that day, and their delay stalled Smith's division, which was waiting to use the same road. Then came the greatest Confederate error of the day. Longstreet on his own initiative decided to leave the Nine Mile Road and use a different approach route than the one he had been assigned. He headed south to the Williamsburg Road, where his long column threw the entire Confederate advance into confusion. During his march he encountered a swollen stream called Gillis Creek, and stopped his command for an hour in order to construct a plank bridge over it. He then sent his men over the bridge in single file! While they were crossing, Huger's division came up and had to wait for its turn to use the ramshackle bridge. Huger's delay in turn stalled Hill's attack, since Hill had been directed not to start battle until Huger came up on his right to relieve his flank guard (Rodes' brigade).

Longstreet's disappearance from the position where he was supposed to be caused confusion all up and down the Confederate front. Whiting, who was leading his troops up the Nine Mile Road as he was directed to do, had been ordered to form on Longstreet's left, but Longstreet was nowhere to be found. This caused Whiting to stop his advance and ask Johnston for instructions. Johnston was at once alarmed and sent a staff officer, Lieutenant J.B. Washington, down the Nine Mile Road to locate Longstreet. The unfortunate Lieutenant found no Confederates in sight and rode right into Keyes' Union lines at Fair Oaks, so alerting the enemy of the pending attack. Shortly thereafter one of Smith's aides arrived to tell Johnston that he had located Longstreet over on the Williamsburg Road. Johnston was flabbergasted, and was heard to mutter "I wish all the troops were back in camp." Nevertheless, he took no positive action to sort out all the confusion. One Confederate artillery officer called the whole situation "incredible" and "almost ludicrous."

Longstreet's mayhem for the day did not stop here. Once his men crossed Gillis Creek, he decided to divide up his division. He sent Pickett's brigade towards the Richmond and York River Railroad and directed three brigades to follow Huger up the Williamsburg Road, while he held his other two brigades in reserve. This mixed up arrangement would keep almost his entire command out of action during the coming battle.

D.H. Hill, meanwhile, was champing at the bit to get the battle started. He had three of his brigades up and ready for action astride the Williamsburg Road at 0600. All he needed to start the battle was the arrival of Rodes' brigade from the Charles City Road on his right. Johnston's battle orders had instructed Huger to relieve Rodes, and Hill was to attack as soon as Rodes came up. Hill waited impatiently all morning for Rodes, not knowing that Longstreet's errors had delayed

Captured Confederate Lieutenant J.B. Washington of Johnston's staff poses with former West Point classmate, Lieutenant George Armstrong Custer. Custer served on McClellan's staff during the Peninsula campaign. By the end of the war he had risen to the rank of major general and was a famous Union hero.

Huger at least five hours. Late in the morning he at last established contact with Longstreet and twice unsuccessfully requested permission to start the attack. At last Rodes' brigade came running up at about 1300, and the battle was finally set to start. Hill ordered three cannons from Bondurant's "Jeff Davis" battery to fire their signal shots, and then launched his assault.

Hill organized his advance along the axis of the Williamsburg Road. He directed Garland to advance north of the road, supported by G.B. Anderson, while Rodes attacked south of the road, supported by Rains. He should not have placed Rodes in the front line since Rodes needed additional time to form his lines after his hurried march from the Charles City Road. As a result, Rodes' advance, as well as Rains', was delayed at least 15 minutes behind the rest of the division. Garland and Anderson were not aware of Rodes' delay, and pushed forward through heavy underbrush and rain swollen bogs until they reached the Union lines.

The battle proper began as Garland's 2,000 man brigade started engaging the enemy alone. The Union line struck by Garland consisted of a full division (Casey's) that stretched a mile from the White Oak Swamp south of the Williamsburg Road northwards to Fair Oaks Station on the railroad. Casey's men had dug shallow rifle pits and felled protective abatis on their front. Their position was anchored on the left by a large redoubt ("Casey's Redoubt") manned by a battery of six Napoleon cannons. Three-quarters of a mile to the rear, Keyes' other division (Couch's) formed a second line north from Seven Pines, also fronted by abatis.

Garland's advance successfully pushed back the Union skirmishers and the *103rd Pennsylvania* that was sent to their support. The Confederates met difficulty crossing the line of abatis and then ran into heavy fire from Spratt's Battery "H" of the *1st New York Artillery* and its three supporting regiments from Naglee's brigade. Garland cried out for support as his 23rd North Carolina lost all of its field officers and the 2nd Florida lost most of its color guard. Finally Anderson came up, and together the two brigades began forcing Naglee's line back.

The battle soon reached a greater intensity along the Williamsburg Road. Rodes committed his regiments to action as they came up, and so did not conduct a coordinated attack at first. His regiments absorbed heavy losses, particularly from the guns in Casey's Redoubt. The troops on the Union left, which had earlier held their fire in order to avoid hitting Naglee's men, opened fire on Rodes' separated units. The commander of the *85th New York* described the action: "We then delivered a continuous volley until they halted, wavered, and turned back. Their color bearer was several times shot down, and when they retreated to the slashing, they lost their colors, along with their dead and wounded."

Rodes dealt with the situation successfully by bringing up Carter's battery to neutralize the guns in Casey's Redoubt. He then ordered Rains to move to the right in order to take the redoubt from the rear. Rains' attack struck home at about 1500, just when Garland and Anderson were breaking through north of the Williamsburg Road. The Yankees held off for a brief 15 minutes before breaking to the rear in confusion. Colonel Guilford Bailey, Couch's chief of artillery, attempted to spike the guns in the redoubt and was felled by a shot that pierced both his temples. Hill's victory became complete as his men seized eight Union cannons plus Casey's entire camp with all its equipment.

Hill sent a messenger to Longstreet to ask for help, since he had not received any of the planned support on either flank. Longstreet did not know the location of Huger's division and his own three brigades sent earlier to the right, and only had two brigades with him in general reserve. He consented to release one of these, R.H. Anderson's, to meet Hill's urgent request. While Anderson came forward, Rodes had to beat back a brief Union counterattack against Casey's Redoubt. It was repulsed with the aid of Carter's battery and some troops who turned the captured Union guns against their former owners.

When R.H. Anderson came up, Hill divided his fresh brigade into two detachments in order to push the advance. The renewed attack made good progress on the left, but on the right it ran into Couch's troops posted strongly at Seven Pines. Hill tried to repeat the tactic he had used successfully

Joseph E. Johnston (left) with Robert E. Lee after the war. When Johnston was wounded at Seven Pines, Lee was given command of the Army of Northern Virginia.

earlier in the day, and sent Rains to swing around the Union left. This time Rains came up short and was stopped by the Union defenses. Rains fell wounded and Rodes' brigade, battered again by a fruitless assault, had to be withdrawn. When Kearny's division of Heintzelman's corps came up, it looked as if the Yankees might regain the day.

It was not to be. Part of R.H. Anderson's brigade stabilized the Confederate right while the left section of the brigade, led by Colonel Micah Jenkins, broke through the Union right near Seven Pines. This caused Couch's line to collapse, and the weary Federals did not reform until they reached a third defensive line manned by more of Heintzelman's troops about one and one-half miles east of Seven Pines. The 5th South Carolina pursued the retreating enemy until 1930, when it was recalled because of a lack of support and approaching darkness.

Longstreet and Hill spent all afternoon wondering when they would receive support from the troops on their left along the Nine Mile Road. In fact, thousands of troops under Generals Whiting and Smith were poised there ready for action, waiting for orders from Johnston to make their attack. Johnston, however, refused to release them until he was certain that Hill had started the battle. Slowly the afternoon rolled on, and Johnston was increasingly concerned that he heard no sounds of battle from Hill's front. Finally, the noise of musketry and artillery was heard about 1600, and he at last sent Smith and Whiting forward.

It seems strange that Johnston was only two or three miles from the scene of Hill's battle at Seven Pines and did not hear the sounds of fighting for three hours. Yet that is precisely what happened. Johnston did not hear Hill's combat because of a condition called "acoustic shadow", an atmospheric phenomenon under which low lying clouds and thick woods combine to muffle sounds or deflect them from traveling in certain directions. This was not the only case of "acoustic shadow" recorded during the war. Other notable instances were at Gaines' Mill later in the Peninsula Campaign, and at Perryville, Kentucky later that fall.

Johnston ordered Whiting's division into action by sending four brigades down the Nine Mile Road while a fifth brigade (Hood's) marched to the right to help Longstreet. Whiting's lead brigade, commanded by Colonel Evander Law, drew near Fair Oaks and spotted a few of Couch's regiments that had been left isolated at this end of the line by Keyes' defeat at Seven Pines. Law turned to face them, and was surprised to fall under strong artillery fire from the north. The firing came from the advance elements of Sedgwick's division of Sumner's *II Corps*. Sumner was well aware of the battle raging at Seven Pines because he was not a victim of "acoustic shadow" and had confirmation from Thaddeus Lowe's observation balloon. He had his engineers build two makeshift bridges across the Chickahominy, one for Richardson's division and one for Sedgwick's. Richardson's proved to be too flimsy to use, and Sedgwick's looked no stronger. It was made of planks set on heavy ropes stretched between large trees on each side of the river; the troops called it the "Grapevine Bridge" or the "Devil's Bridge." At 1430 Sumner sent Sedgwick's men across: "The column is in motion and moves to the log-way with a quick step as officers of the group watch with breathless anxiety the effect it will have on the loose and swinging structure. Doubt and anxiety soon changes into a feeling of joy. It is found that the weight of the advancing column presses the loose timbers down, fastens them, as it were, to the stumps and mud; and indeed increases the strength and solidity of the swinging mass. A half suppressed cheer now relieves many a heart of its burden. Never before did an army cross a stream under such disheartening circumstances."

Troops of Sumner's **II Corps** *advance south across the swollen Chickahominy River during the battle of Seven Pines. Sumner's timely arrival on the beleaguered right helped defeat Johnston's only major attack during the Peninsula campaign.*

Observation Balloons

The use of hot air and gas filled balloons was another novelty of the Civil War. The science of aeronautics had been developed in the early 1850s in Europe and was brought to the United States primarily by Thaddeus S.C. Lowe (1832-1913), a native of New Hampshire who was fascinated by the subject and went to France to study it in 1854. Lowe made his first American ascension in 1858, and the next year built an elaborate areostat, the *City of New York*, for the purpose of trans-Atlantic travel. Mechanical difficulties, though, caused the balloon to malfunction. Lowe's first successful long range flight was in the 20,000 cubic foot *Commercial*, which took off from Cincinnati on 20 April 1861 and headed southeast at an unheard of 100 miles per hour. He landed the next day in Unionville, South Carolina, and expected a hero's welcome. Instead, he was thrown in jail as a Northern spy— Fort Sumter had fallen just the week before, and he had to be rescued by friends from the scientific community.

Upon his release, Lowe offered his services to the United States government. No one questioned the military potential of balloons, but the government gave its contract to a Pennsylvanian named John Wise. Wise took his balloon with McDowell's army to Bull Run, only to see it punctured by tree branches before it could be in-flated. Upon hearing of Wise's misfortune, Lincoln at once recalled Lowe and sent him to his secretary of war, who refused to see the aeronaut until the president came with him personally. Lowe was then hired to set up a balloon corps, receiving the pay of a colonel.

Lowe eventually constructed seven observation balloons for military use, ranging from 15,000 to 32,000 cubic feet. The balloons were constructed by a double thickness of India silk, oiled on the inside to be pliable and were covered with four coats of varnish on the outside for durability. Lowe found gas to be much more reliable than hot air and developed his own field generators. Altogether he and his balloons made over 3,000 ascensions during the first two years of the war. Lowe became quite proficient at spotting enemy camps and troop movements, and was even successful at directing artillery fire by using a telegraphic wire that stretched up about a mile to his balloon tethered in the sky.

Lowe's balloon corps was at its best during the Peninsula campaign. His balloons detected Johnston's withdrawal from Yorktown on 5 May, and Lowe personally observed many of the Confederate movements during the battle of Seven Pines (31 May-1 June). Later in the campaign, he successfully used a balloon tethered to a boat in the James River. McClellan was much impressed with the information the balloons furnished, but major General Fitz-John Porter, commander of the *V Corps*, may have held a different opinion of them after a wild escapade he experienced in front of Yorktown on 11 April 1862. It seems that when he went up in a balloon for an observation for himself, he left so hastily that only one tethering rope was ready. When this broke the astonished general found himself adrift in the sky. It was much to his good fortune that the wind happened to be from the northwest and carried him away from the enemy lines; otherwise he would have been captured and gravely embarrassed. At length he managed to release the balloon's gas valve, and the wayward balloon eventually came to the ground by crashing into a large tent amidst the hurrahs of the soldiers and a band that arrived for the occasion.

Lowe contracted malaria during the Peninsula campaign and was unable to go aloft during the Second Bull Run and Antietam campaigns, where his services would have been most useful. He at last returned to action late in 1862 and provided important observations at Fredericksburg in December 1862 and at Chancellorsville in May 1863. Unfortunately, weather conditions prohibited him from going aloft on 2 May 1863, when he probably would have detected "Stonewall" Jackson's march against Hooker's exposed right flank and perhaps might have changed the course of the battle.

In spite of Lowe's meritorious service, Hooker reorganized and degraded the balloon corps after Chancellorsville. This angered Lowe so much that he resigned on 8 May 1863, and his balloons became unused curiosities. Lowe returned to his primary love, scientific invention, after the war. He developed a form of refrigerator coolant and also established Lowe Observatory in Pasadena, California.

The Confederates also used balloons, but they did not make as many as the Federals because of their lack of technological resources. The best Confederate balloons were developed at Richmond, where the Richmond Gas Works provided a reliable source of inflating gas. Captain E. Porter Alexander, later a noted artillerist, made numerous ascensions during the Peninsula campaign. The most noted balloon was the "silk dress" balloon used during the Seven Days Battles. (It was not really made from donated dresses, as legend records, but from new fabric.) This balloon was tethered to a Confederate boat named *Teaser* that was anchored in the James River. It made numerous ascensions from 27 June 1862 until the first week of July, when it was captured after the *Teaser* ran aground. Another silk balloon was built in Charleston, South Carolina, in the spring of 1863 by a contracted civilian aeronaut, Charles Cevor. When it was carried off by a sudden high wind, the Confederate aeronautic corps passed into history also.

After crossing, Sumner formed up four brigades at the Adams House, three-quarters of a mile northeast of Fair Oaks Station. When Whiting's Confederate troops began to come up late in the afternoon, G.W. Smith, Whiting's superior, arrived to take charge and sent two brigades, Pettigrew's and Hampton's, to attack Sumner's line. It was a splendid attack, only to be mowed down by the Union guns. Pettigrew fell wounded, and the Confederates ran for cover. Hatton's Tennessee brigade came up to stabilize the line just as the Federals mounted a counterattack. Hatton was killed, Hampton fell wounded, and the fighting continued on between the two sides that were about evenly matched at 9,000 men each.

The firing began to die down by mutual consent as darkness settled. Johnston decided that the troops should sleep on their arms in order to be able to renew the conflict at dawn, and rode forward at 1830 to give the order to his commands. It was a dangerous and momentous decision to ride to the front. Johnston describes what occurred: "About seven o'clock I received a slight wound in my right shoulder from a musket shot, and, a few moments after, was unhorsed by a heavy fragment of shell which struck my breast. Those round had me borne from the field in an ambulance; not, however, before the President, who was with General Lee not far in the rear, had heard of the accident and visited me, manifesting great concern."

Davis came up just as Johnston was regaining consciousness. He later wrote that Johnston "opened his eyes, smiled, and gave me his hand, said he did not know how seriously he had been hurt, but feared a fragment of shell had hurt his spine." As Johnston regained his senses, his greatest concern was that he has lost his sidearms, consisting of two pistols and a sword. "That sword," he said, "was the one worn by my father in the Revolutionary War, and I would not lose it for $10,000; will not somebody please go back and get it and the pistol for me." One of the general's couriers, Drury Armistead, volunteered for the mission, even though enemy fire had become heavier in the area. He found the sword and pistols at the spot when Johnston had been wounded, and returned them safely. The thankful general presented his aide with one of the pistols in gratitude for the favor.

The "Gray Fox," Robert E. Lee. Before he took command of the Army of Northern Virginia, Lee was scorned by many politicians, fellow generals and troops. After defeating McClellan, Lee was a virtual living Southern icon beloved by civilians and soldiers alike.

CHAPTER VIII

Lee Takes Command

*T*he wounding of Confederate General Joe Johnston at about 1900 on 31 May 1862 changed the course of the war, though no one knew it at the time. As the wounded general was being conveyed to Richmond, President Jefferson Davis, who had been at the front with his military advisor, General Robert E. Lee, found Major General G.W. Smith, the army's senior division commander, and turned command of the army over to him. Davis asked Smith what his intentions would be, and the general outlined Johnston's battle plan and how it had gone awry during the day. Smith added that he had carried out his part of the operation but did not know what was happening on Longstreet's front. Until he learned the situation on the right, he could not determine what was best to do next.

Smith's responses were not totally satisfactory to Davis, and the president discussed the situation with Lee as the two rode back to Richmond. Davis was also concerned about leaving Smith in command of the army, since he did not get along well with him personally. Furthermore, the general seemed diffident and exhausted; Smith would in fact suffer a physical breakdown two days later. Sometime during their ride back to Richmond, Davis made the momentous decision to turn control of the army over to Lee. The two understood each other well, and Lee was quite familiar with the army and its problems from his role as personal military advisor to the president. In addition, Lee's rank as full general made him senior to Smith and all the other division commanders. Most importantly, Lee was very experienced and very available for duty, since he was only manning an office in Richmond. Reportedly Davis said to his advisor, "General Lee, I shall assign you to command of this army. Make your preparations as soon as you reach your quarters. I shall send you the order when I get to Richmond." This appointment may have been the best decision Davis would make during the war.

It seems odd that Lee did not at once return to the front, since the battle was certain to be renewed at dawn. He instead went home, which he probably reached by midnight. He may have gotten four or five hours of sleep before he was awakened at 0500 by a courier from Smith, who reported the general's battle plans and requested reinforcements and some engineers. Lee responded supportingly to Smith and addressed him in a note as "Cmdg. Army of N.Va." A short while later Lee received a communication from Davis that concluded, "You will assume command of the armies in Eastern Virginia and in North Carolina, and give orders as may be needful and proper." He was now officially the commander of the army that was engaged in a fierce battle only a few miles away, yet he continued to do paperwork and did not leave for the front until 1300. This, too, seems most strange, and Lee never explained the reason for his delay at assuming command. He probably felt that Smith had the situation under control, and that his presence on the field might interfere with the plans Smith was enacting.

Smith, meanwhile, spent the night trying to learn all he could about the army's position. All he knew for certain was that the enemy was close by his front and that the battle would most likely be renewed in the morning. He had no idea what had happened on Longstreet's front until cavalry commander Jeb Stuart arrived. He reported that there had been no Confederate advance on the Charles City Road, and that D.H. Hill had captured Seven Pines and proceeded some distance beyond. At length Longstreet came up around 0100 and confirmed Stuart's report. He and Smith then conferred for over an hour. Smith wanted Longstreet to use Whiting's fresh troops for support and renew the battle on his front. Longstreet was not inclined to do so because of the heavy reinforcements Keyes had received (from Heintzelman's corps). After more discussion, Smith altered his proposal and directed Longstreet to attack at dawn in the direction of Fair Oaks. Smith did not elect to attack on his own front because he was aware that the Yankees there were being heavily reinforced. In this he was correct, as Sumner soon after dark had brought up Richardson's division and placed it along the railroad on Sedgwick's left. Smith hoped that Longstreet's morning attack would strike Sumner's exposed left flank, and had no way of knowing that Richardson had already connected his line with Birney's brigade of the *III Corps* which had advanced to within three-quarters of a mile of Fair Oaks. Birney's troops, in turn, connected on their left with the rest of the *III Corps*, which was formed in support of the line that the defeated *IV Corps* had taken up the previous evening. Smith was also concerned that the enemy might use pontoons to build new bridges over the Chickahominy on his left, and advance to flank his army or threaten Richmond.

Longstreet did not form any elaborate plans for battle when he left Smith. He returned to his headquarters at 0300 for an hour of much needed sleep. Then he found D.H. Hill (who had taken over General Casey's abandoned headquarters tent) and began explaining the army's situation to him. During their conference they were startled by several bullets that came whizzing through their tent; some raw Confederate troops had become alarmed by a disturbance in the direction of the Union lines and let go a volley in the wrong direction! Longstreet gave Hill no specific instructions other than to attack to the north and send one of Huger's brigades up to the Nine Mile Road. His parting words to Hill were simply, "You have taken the bull by the horns and must fight him out."

Hill was not one to avoid a good fight, and soon took charge of all the front line troops on that wing, including four

TACTICAL MAP OF BATTLE OF SEVEN PINES

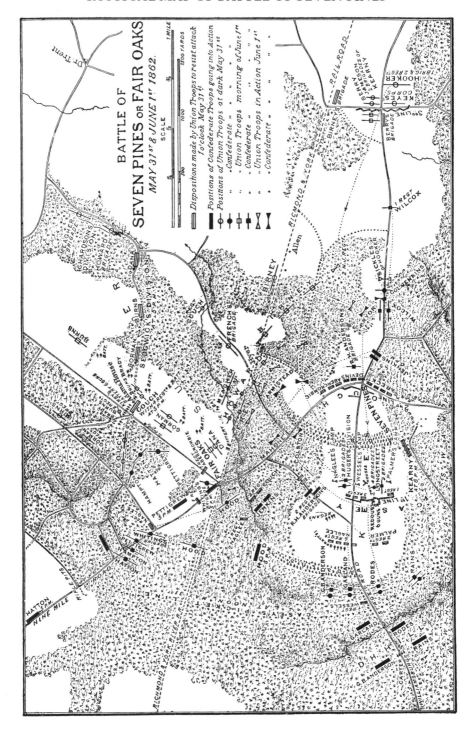

BATTLE OF
SEVEN PINES or FAIR OAKS
MAY 31ST & JUNE 1ST 1862.

SCALE

Dispositions made by Union Troops to resist attack
10 o'clock May 31st
Positions of Confederate Troops going into action
Positions of Union Troops going into action May 31st
Confederate " " " " "
Union Troops morning of June 1st
Confederate " " " " "
Union Troops in Action June 1st
Confederate " " " "

fresh brigades of Longstreet's division and two from Huger's. The fighting was renewed around 0600 when Hill sent Pickett's and Armistead's brigades to attack Sumner's left. Since the Yankees had formed a continuous line at Fair Oaks, the two Confederate brigades were unable to locate any exposed enemy flank and were repulsed. The Federals even mounted a counterattack that routed Armistead's command. Hill threw Mahone's green brigade in to plug the hole, only to see this command, too, fall back. This caused Hill to exchange such heated words with Mahone that the brigadier challenged him to a duel two days later; Mahone was persuaded to drop the challenge, but the two generals would remain personal enemies for the rest of their days.

Undeterred, Hill pushed forward yet another fresh brigade (Colston's) and was dismayed to find that it, too, could not hold its position. Hill did not know that he had struck Richardson's division head on, and Richardson had three large fresh brigades ready to fight. One of the Union brigade commanders reported, "The whole line along the railroad for nearly a mile seemed to have become one continuous blaze of musketry." This intense Union fire power made it impossible for Hill's brigades to close for an attack or even maintain a forward position. Only Pickett's brigade held firm, supported by another regiment or two on each flank. Thus the fighting continued all morning. Towards noon the Yankees mounted a counterattack. Pickett's men by then were running low on ammunition and had to give way. During this attack Union Brigadier General Oliver O. Howard, future commander of the *Army of the Tennessee*, received two serious wounds that resulted in the amputation of his right arm.

The fighting was dying down about 1330 when President Davis rode up to Smith's headquarters near Old Tavern. It was an awkward moment. Davis at once asked for Lee, and was extremely surprised to learn that he was not there. Davis then told Smith that "early in the morning he had ordered General Lee to take command of the army at once." Smith

Lee's Horses

In the spring of 1861, General Robert E. Lee had as his mount a bay stallion named "Richmond," which had been given to him by friends. The animal turned out to have a nervous disposition, and would squeal whenever he was around unfamiliar horses. Lee wrote about him, "He is a troublesome fellow, and dislikes to associate with strange horses. He expresses it more in words than acts, and if firmly treated becomes quiet at last." When Lee went on his campaign in western Virginia that fall, he found it necessary to obtain a second mount, which he called simply "Brown Roan." In early 1862, the general obtained a third mount named "Jeff Davis" or "Greenbrier," the latter name from the western Virginia county where the animal was raised. "Jeff Davis" was four years old and iron gray in color, and first had been seen by Lee during his Sewell Mountain campaign in western Virginia.

Lee apparently used all three of his horses during the Seven Days Battles, though "Roan" was beginning to go blind at the time. When "Richmond" died soon after the battle of Malvern Hill and the ailing "Roan" was given to the care of a local farmer, Lee took up "Greenbrier", now renamed "Traveller" (in the British spelling) , as his primary mount. The horse had a fast walk and a short, high trot (called a "buck trot") that made him difficult to ride, but Lee was a superb horseman and so had no difficulty at managing him. "Traveler" carried his master well through the rigors of the war, with one notable exception. On 31 August 1862, the day after the great battle of Second Bull Run ended in another Confederate victory, Lee was riding "Traveller" in a reconnaissance. At one point, the general dismounted to direct some troops, with "Traveller" an arm's length away. Suddenly a cry of "Enemy cavalry!" was heard. "Traveller" was startled by the commotion, and jumped as Lee grabbed for his reins. This caused Lee to trip and fall forward. The general used his hands to break his fall, and in the process sprained one hand and broke a small bone in the other hand. Since both of his hands had to be set in splints by a doctor, Lee was unable to ride and had to direct most of the ensuing Antietam campaign from the back of an army ambulance. Because of this incident, cavalry commander Jeb Stuart gave

must surely have been taken aback, since this was the first news he had of Lee's appointment. At least it was no rumor, as he heard the news directly from Davis himself. Smith com-

Lee a five-year-old mare of more quiet disposition named "Lucy Long." Lee rode her whenever his hands hurt or when "Traveller" needed rest. "Lucy Long" was retired when the army was at Petersburg because she "got with foal". In late 1862 Lee was also given a sorrel named "Ajax," which he used only occasionally because he was too tall for the general to ride comfortably.

Lee grew to be quite fond of "Traveller", despite the animal's strange gait. The general once described his favorite mount to an artist who wanted to do a portrait of "Traveller": "If I were an artist like you, I would draw a true picture of Traveller, representing his fine proportions, muscular figure, deep chest, short back, strong haunches, flat legs, small head, broad forehead, delicate ears, quick eye, small feet and black mane and tail. Such a picture would inspire a poet, whose genius could then depict his worth and describe his endurance of toil, hunger, thirst, heat and cold, and the dangers and sufferings through which he has passed. He could dilate upon his sagacity and his affection, and invariable response to every wish of his rider. I am no artist, and can therefore say that he is a Confederate gray."

"Traveller, "Lucy Long," and "Ajax" accompanied General Lee to Lexington after the war when he became president of Washington College. "Ajax" died a few years later when he ran into the iron prong of a gate latch. "Traveller" and "Lucy Long" both survived the general, who died in 1870. "Traveller" passed away from lockjaw not long after his master, and was buried at Washington and Lee University. His bones for some reason were disinterred in 1907, and the skeleton was displayed in a museum at the school until they were at length reburied near the chapel where General Lee and his family were interred. "Traveller's" saddle and other gear are on display at the Museum of the Confederacy in Richmond. "Traveller" is the protagonist in a cute and well written 1988 novel by Richard Adams, appropriately entitled *Traveller*, which gives the war from a horse's point of view.

The last survivor of General Lee's horses was "Lucy Long." She had been stolen during the last days of the war, but was found in the eastern part of the state and was returned to the general. In 1878 she cut her legs badly while running loose on the campus of Washington College. She was then sent to some farmers in Rockbridge County to be cared for. She died there in 1891 or shortly afterwards, being over 34 years old.

posed himself quickly and responded, "In that case he will probably soon be here." He invited Davis to come into his headquarters to wait. The president "did so and chatted pleasantly upon a variety of common-place subjects, but made no allusion to anything pertaining to the state of affairs upon the field."

Davis' awkward visit continued for half an hour until Lee rode up about 1400. Lee rightly assumed that Davis had already announced the change of command, and calmly took control of the situation. After Smith briefed him on the army's condition, the two generals rode over to the Williamsburg Road to see Longstreet. Longstreet expressed anger that he had received no support from Whiting on his left, and reported that he was under attack on his right by Union troops that were farther down the Williamsburg Road. This last information convinced Lee that the enemy had been heavily reinforced all along his line, so he ordered Longstreet to break off the engagement and withdraw to his former lines.

Lee's decision brought an end to the two day long battle known to the Confederates as Seven Pines (where they had their greatest success on 31 May) and to the Federals as Fair Oaks (where they had their greatest success on 1 June). The Union generals did not follow up on Longstreet's withdrawal, since they lacked an overall front line commander— McClellan was sick with a fever and was not able to come to the front until the fighting was ended. Even then, he looked pale and quite unwell. For a short time he discussed with General Porter, the commander of his *V Corps*, the possibility of bringing the whole army across the Chickahominy to pursue the Confederates to Richmond. Porter, however, objected to the plan because of the unreliability of the bridges over the river. McClellan was too ill to consider the matter further, and went back to his headquarters to return to bed. He was so sick that he could not ride a horse for 10 days.

Thus neither side gained any advantage from the battle. On 31 May the Confederates had an excellent chance to destroy one or two of McClellan's corps, but a number of factors intervened to keep them from changing the course of the campaign—Longstreet's errors, the wounding of Johnston,

The remnants of battle. Federals bury their dead and burn the corpses of horses in the wake of the battle of Seven Pines. The Federals lost about 5,000 troops in the two-day battle. The Confederates suffered some 6,000 casualties.

Smith's indecisiveness, and Sumner's bold crossing of the Grapevine Bridge. Most of the errors in the battle were made by the commanders. The troops as a whole fought well in what was the first combat for most of them. The Confederates as the aggressors suffered more casualties (6,134, including 980 killed and 4,749 wounded) than did the Federals (5,031 casualties, including 790 killed and 3,594 wounded). Both sides had about 41,800 men on the field. Besides these losses, the only important result of the battle was Robert E. Lee's accession to command the "Army of Northern Virginia," as he christened his new command on 1 June.

Lee had a number of important matters to deal with after he pulled his troops backs from Seven Pines. The most immediate question was whether to hold the army where it was or pull it back closer to Richmond. Upon conferring with Long-street, Lee decided to maintain the army where it was in hopes that this would force McClellan to keep the Union army astride the Chickahominy; this awkward Federal position offered Lee the opportunity to strike either enemy wing if he wished. There was no opportunity, however, for either side to do much maneu-vering in the week following Seven Pines as the heavens contin-ued to pour down shower after shower. The roads continued to be so bad that Major General Ambrose Burnside, who was visiting the Union army, said that it took him four and one-half hours just to ride nine miles.

The week of inaction gave Lee the needed opportunity to get to know his army better. On 2 June he called his generals together to hear their concerns. Some of Johnston's cronies were annoyed that a "staff officer" had been put in command, and several of the division commanders did not like to see the brigadiers invited to the meeting. Lee listened patiently to everyone and began the process of developing a personal understanding of each of his generals. Soon he would gain everyone's trust and confidence by his energy, tact and self assurance. This good relationship with all his officers would be a key factor in the army's successes the next three years. Another of Lee's strengths was that he understood President Davis well and had his full confidence, something Johnston had not shared.

Lee also needed to establish a relationship with the troops of his new army. Most of the men had no idea who their new commander was, though they were curious to see what he looked like and to learn his qualities. Their immediate reac-tion to him was not positive. Lee at once set most of them to work felling trees, digging trenches, and constructing fortifi-cations. This was all considered "Negro's work", not activities fit for white soldiers. Furthermore, the troops much preferred to face the enemy in the open "like men" rather than fire from a hole in the dirt. They definitely did not appreciate the value of trenches then as much as they would later in the war. For the moment they simply complained about all the digging and derisively called Lee the "King of Spades".

Lee had a definite reason for constructing all his fortifications—and it was not in order to be ready for the siege that McClellan seemed ready to start. Lee knew that acquiescing to a Federal siege would surely mean defeat because of enemy superiority in numbers and in heavy artillery. The purpose of the trenches was to be able to defend Richmond with as few troops as possible so that he might be able to take the offensive with the rest.

Lee's first offensive plans were based on "Stonewall" Jackson's successful operations in the Shenandoah Valley. If Jackson were reinforced, he would be able to conduct an invasion of Pennsylvania that might force Lincoln to recall McClellan from Richmond. Lee, however, did not have sufficient troops to spare for Jackson, since his entrenchments were not yet finished. Lee was aware, from his earlier service in Georgia and South Carolina, that there were a number of brigades stationed along the Atlantic coast that President Davis might call forward to Virginia. Davis made the call, only to be thwarted by every district commander and governor from North Carolina to Florida. All feared Yankee incursions and would not release any of their troops. The only significant reinforcements Lee would receive from that quarter would be Lawton's fine Georgia brigade, which was already en route.

Lee understood that he would not be able to send Jackson enough men to enable "Stonewall" to invade the North. Instead, he would use Jackson to make a more daring attack— against McClellan's right flank. Lee was well aware that McClellan's left flank was anchored on White Oak Swamp, while his right was vulnerable in more open ground near Mechanicsville. If Jackson were brought down secretly from the Valley while McClellan's army still straddled the Chickahominy, Lee would be able to crush the Union right and then perhaps capture McClellan's supply base at White House, so putting an end to the campaign.

The opportunity for Lee to carry out this strategy was presented after Jackson skillfully defeated Fremont at Cross Keyes on 8 June then vanquished Shields at Port Republic on 9 June. Lee was very much aware that Jackson's victories would persuade Lincoln to keep McDowell's command from joining McClellan, and that is exactly what happened; of McDowell's three divisions slated to be sent to the Peninsula, only one, McCall's, actually arrived. In order to heighten the impression that Jackson was going to do more mischief in the Valley, Lee sent him three brigades of reinforcements—Lawton's, which had just reached Richmond from Georgia, and Whiting's two brigades. All were sent off with much fanfare on 11 June. Lee wanted to be sure that the newspapers—and Abraham Lincoln—would be aware that Jackson's being heavily reinforced. These troops would actually return with Jackson as soon as the details of Lee's strategy were worked out. Meanwhile, Jackson needed a few days to rest his men after the rigors of their Valley campaign. Lee also needed to verify the position of McClellan's army and its supports, which he did by sending Jeb Stuart in his famous raid around the Union army on 12-15 June (see sidebar).

McClellan had indeed left his right flank open to an attack when he moved his army closer to Richmond in mid-June. The army had not done much in the days following Seven Pines because of McClellan's illness and the horribly rainy weather. By mid-month the engineers had new bridges erected over the swollen Chickahominy, and McClellan sent Franklin's *VI Corps* to join Sumner's, Keyes' and Heintzelman's troops in the lines they had occupied since Seven Pines. McClellan's intention was to advance along the line of the Richmond and York River Railroad as soon as the ground dried out. He had left only one corps, Porter's *V*, on the north side of the Chickahominy in order to guard the approaches to the army's supply base at White House. Porter was also well positioned to link up with McDowell's command, should that force be authorized to advance south from the Fredericksburg area. Porter was strongly posted on the hills behind Beaver Dam Creek, which flowed into the Chickahominy near Mechanicsville. McClellan did not fear for Porter's security since he had reinforced the *V Corps* with McCall's excellent division of the Pennsylvania Reserves, which had just arrived from McDowell's command. McCall's troops and other reinforcements more than made up for army's casualties at Seven Pines and losses to disease.

On 20 June McClellan reported 127,327 men in his army, of whom about 104,000 were ready for duty. His belief that the Confederates had 180,000 (they actually had less than 65,000) strengthened his conviction that only a siege would effect the capture of Richmond. He was pleased that the rains finally quit towards the end of the month, so that the ground would begin to dry enough to support his heavy guns. On 24 June he gave orders for Heintzelman's corps to make a limited advance from Seven Pines. From that position Heintzelman would in turn support an advance that Franklin would make the next day to Old Tavern, located four miles in advance of Seven Pines and less than three miles from Richmond. The decisive stage of the battle for Richmond was about to begin—but not on ground of McClellan's choosing.

Lee's Lieutenants

Confederate General Robert E. Lee inherited a mixed bag of commanders from Joe Johnston when he took over would be the Army of Northern Virginia on 1 June 1862. Some of the army's senior officers proved to be too old for field service, while others were inflexible or difficult to deal with. In addition, most had not seen combat before the battle of Seven Pines, and their combat ability had to be evaluated as well as their administrative skills. Lee was a good judge of character, and in the three weeks before he entered the Seven Days Battles he rearranged the army and its commanders as best he could. The army and its officers still, however, would need more fine tuning before reaching their peak of efficiency.

The Confederate army of approximately 11 divisions was not formally divided into corps or wings because of a law prohibiting the appointment of officers above the rank of major general. This situation definitely would hamper the army's efficiency. At various stages of the campaign "ad hoc" commands were created, but these were transient and their subunits interchangeable. For example, Longstreet had charge of the Confederate rear guard at Williamsburg and then led the Confederate right at Seven Pines (though D.H. Hill did all the fighting at the front) before overseeing A.P. Hill in the last stages of the campaign.

G.W. Smith led the Confederate left at Seven Pines, and Jackson during the Seven Days Battles commanded a growing force that eventually included four divisions—his own, Ewell's, Whiting's and D.H. Hill's. During the campaign Magruder and Huger also commanded divisional groupings.

None of the Confederate commanders performed without flaw during the campaign. The performance of "Stonewall" Jackson (1824-1863, West Point Class of 1846) was enigmatic and totally disappointing. He was probably suffering from exhaustion after his demanding spring campaign in the Shenandoah Valley, and was disoriented in unfamiliar terrain around Richmond (see sidebar). Jackson would win eternal fame for his generalship at Second Bull Run, Antietam and Chancellorsville. He was not idolized before his death as much as he is today. Much of the adulation did not begin until after he was mortally wounded at Chancellorsville (where he was accidentally shot by his own men) and became a martyr to the Southern cause.

Major General James Longstreet (1821-1904, West Point Class of 1842) performed well as Confederate rear guard commander at Williamsburg, and then had perhaps his worst battle of the war at Seven Pines, where he was nominally the wing commander but let D.H. Hill handle all the fighting.

In addition, his decision to take the wrong road to the battlefield totally ruined Johnston's battle plan for the day. Longstreet later became Lee's most trusted corps commander and the army's second-in-command. His controversial role at Gettysburg is still debated. Longstreet yearned for the opportunity to hold independent command, but performed poorly when given the opportunity at Suffolk and Knoxville in 1863. After the war he became a Republican, an act that turned most of the old South against him, and he had to defend his military career in his memoirs, *From Manassas to Appomattox* (1896).

Lee's best fighting general in the campaign was Major General Daniel Harvey Hill (1821-1889, West Point Class of 1842), a brother-in-law of "Stonewall" Jackson. Hill fought aggressively at Seven Pines, Mechanicsville, and Gaines' Mill, and gallantly defended the Sunken Road at Antietam. His fighting qualities, however, were lost to the army when Lee had to transfer him to North Carolina because of his acerbic personality and his inability to get along with many of his fellow officers.

Major General Ambrose Powell Hill (1825-1865, West Point Class of 1847) was also a superior fighter. "The Other Hill" was no relation to D.H. Hill. "Powell," as he was called, led his newly formed "Light Division" with skill throughout the Seven Days Battles. He was a fine division officer, but did not perform well as commander of the Third Corps, par-

ticularly at Gettysburg. Hill was high strung (modern scholars believe he may have suffered from a venereal disease) and often argued with his fellow officers, including Longstreet and Jackson. He usually wore a red shirt into battle, and was killed in action near Petersburg on 2 April 1865 during the last week of the war.

Major General Richard S. Ewell (1817-1872, West Point Class of 1840) was another skilled division commander who was later promoted beyond his ability level. He fought well under Jackson in the Valley and performed adequately during the Seven Days Battles. He lost a leg at Groveton in August 1862 and afterwards had to be strapped to his saddle in order to ride in the field. When he returned to action he had lost much of his aggressiveness and could not live up to expectations as Jackson's successor to the command of the *II Corps* after Chancellorsville. His indecision on the evening of 1 July 1863 may have cost Lee a victory at Gettysburg. Ewell held command until he was disabled by a fall from his horse at Spotsylvania in May 1864.

Major General Gustavus W. Smith (1822-1896, West Point Class of 1842) was a promising officer who did not achieve his potential because of physical problems—he suffered from bouts of paralysis, especially when under stress. He commanded a division at Yorktown and then led the Confederate left wing at Seven Pines. He did not really know what to do with the army when he inherited it for

18 hours after Joe Johnston was wounded on the evening of 31 May 1862. Lee succeeded him as army commander on 1 June and relieved him of duty the next day because Smith was exhausted and suffering another attack of paralysis. Smith held a number of minor positions later in the war, the most significant of which was acting secretary of war for a few days in November 1863.

Lee was faced with a problem determining the successor to Smith's division command when Smith was relieved on 2 June 1862. Smith's senior brigadier was H.W.C. Whiting (1824-1865), who had performed very well at Eltham's Landing and led the division while Smith was wing and army commander at Seven Pines. Whiting, however, had a sour and pessimistic attitude and Lee found him difficult to work with. Lee resolved the problem by reducing Smith's old division to two brigades and then sending Whiting to join Jackson's command; Smith's other three brigades were transferred to A.P. Hill's command in order to create the "Light Division." Lee transferred Whiting to North Carolina later in 1862, where he was mortally wounded and captured at Fort Fisher on 15 January 1865.

Lee also had a personality conflict with Benjamin Huger (1805-1877, West Point Class of 1825), the commander of the old Norfolk garrison. Huger was crusty and uncooperative, and his troops did not perform especially well at Seven Pines or Frayser's Farm. Modern scholars believe that he may have been suffering from hardening of the arteries. Whatever was the case, Lee had him transferred from Virginia. Huger spent the rest of the war serving as an inspector for the ordnance department and in other minor posts.

Major General Theophilus Holmes (1804-1880) was also old and difficult to deal with. He led a division under Huger's command, and fought only at Malvern Hill during the Seven Days Battles. For some reason he was appointed lieutenant general in command of the Trans-Mississippi Department in the fall of 1862. He took the post only at the urging of his friend, President Jefferson Davis, but was soon relieved at his own request and replaced by Kirby Smith.

Lee also found that Major General John B. Magruder (1810-1871, West Point Class of 1830) did not have exceptional military skills. Magruder, who was known as "Prince John" because of his demeanor and pre-war ability to give fine parties, was at his best when bluffing a stronger opponent, as he did in the first days at Yorktown and when he held the Confederate right to cover Richmond during the battles of Mechanicsville and Gaines' Mill. His performance later in the Seven Days Battles (when he was suffering from a stomach ailment and exhaustion) and thereafter proved disappointing, so Lee transferred him to the District of Texas. Magruder refused to surrender at the end of the war and crossed the Rio Grande to become a major general in the army of the Emperor Maximilian.

Magruder's "command," as it was called, during the Seven Days Battles actually consisted of three "mini-divisions" of two brigades each. One was led by Magruder himself while the second was commanded by Brigadier General David R. Jones (1825-1863, West Point Class of 1846). Jones was a competent officer who fought well until he suffered a heart attack after the battle of Antietam. He died of heart trouble in January 1863. Magruder's third "mini-division" was led by Major General Lafayette McLaws (1821-1897, West Point Class of 1842). McLaws was a solid commander until he was relieved by Longstreet for a lack of cooperation during the Knoxville campaign in late 1863.

The real strength of Lee's army lay perhaps in the enthusiasm and skill of his brigade commanders. Two of the most aggressive were Brigadier Generals John B. Hood and Robert E. Rodes. Hood's charge at Gaines' Mill probably won the battle. He would later lose an arm at Gettysburg and a leg at Chickamauga on his rise to the rank of full general. Hood succeeded Joe Johnston as commander of the Army of Tennessee during the Atlanta campaign and then saw his command virtually destroyed at Franklin and Nashville during his ill-advised invasion of Tennessee in late 1864. Rodes would be an exceptional division level commander until he met death at Winchester in October 1864. Three of Lee's Brigadier Generals during the Seven Days Battles would later rise to the rank of lieutenant general—Richard Taylor, R.H. Anderson and Wade Hampton. Other talented brigadiers who would later rise to division command included George Pickett, Cadmus Wilcox, Robert Ransom, Charles Field, Isaac Trimble, and Charles Winder. Jubal Early, who would succeed Ewell as commander of Jackson's Second Corps, was wounded at Williamsburg and missed the Seven Days Battles.

137

Stuart's First Ride around McClellan

James Ewell Brown ("Jeb") Stuart (1833-1864, West Point Class of 1854) is well known as one of the war's greatest cavalry commanders. His pre-war experience included service against the Indians (where he was badly wounded) and in Kansas. He was an aide to Colonel Robert E. Lee when John Brown was captured at Harpers Ferry in 1859. At the start of the Civil War in 1861 Stuart was commissioned a lieutenant colonel of infantry but transferred to the cavalry just two weeks later. He led his regiment, the 1st Virginia Cavalry, aggressively at First Bull Run and was appointed brigadier general in September 1861. During the Peninsula Campaign he commanded a strong brigade that included seven regiments and four battalions.

In mid-June 1862 General Robert E. Lee wanted to conduct an attack on the right flank of McClellan's Union army that had approached to within six miles of Richmond. Lee's plan was to assault the Union troops posted near Mechanicsville along Beaver Dam Creek, but before he could order the movement he badly needed to know how far north the Union flank extended, and whether or not the Yankee troops occupied the important ridge north of the Chickahominy River near Totopotomoy Creek. On 10 June Lee called Stuart to his headquarters on Nine Mile Road and proposed that the

cavalryman conduct a reconnaissance of McClellan's right. Stuart embraced the idea enthusiastically, and even offered to ride around the entire Union army. Lee, however, clearly did not have this object in mind when he issued Stuart his written instructions the next day: "you will return as soon as the object of your expedition is accomplished, and you must bear constantly in mind, while endeavoring to execute the general purpose of your mission, not to hazard unnecessarily your command...You must leave sufficient cavalry here for the service of this army, and remember that one of the chief objects of your expedition is to gain intelligence for the guidance of future operations."

Later that day Stuart handpicked a select force of 1,200 men for the operation—Colonel Fitzhugh Lee's 1st Virginia, Rooney Lee's 9th Virginia, eight companies of the 4th Virginia, 250 men of the Jeff Davis Legion, the South Carolina Boykin Rangers, and two guns of the Stuart Horse Artillery under Lieutenant Jim Breathed. He did not notify these troops of their mission until 0200 on 12 June, when he awakened them and set them on their way in secrecy.

Stuart's column headed straight north out of Richmond on the Brook Turnpike and covered 22 miles before encamping near Taylorsville and the South Anna River. The force set out at daylight on Friday, 13 June, for its first objective at Hanover Court House. Word came from his scouts (who included famed raider John S. Mosby) that there was a Union force in the town. Stuart sent the 1st Virginia to swing in from the south side of town and gave it time to get into position before leading the rest of his troops in a charge from the west. This attack flushed out a small Union cavalry command, but the 1st Virginia was unable to close the trap—it had been slowed down by a marsh and did not cut off the Yankees' escape route in time.

The enemy had now been alerted to his presence, so Stuart had to proceed quickly as well as cautiously. He was still not nearly as concerned about enemy scouts and patrols as he was with locating prepared positions that might block Lee's proposed flank attack. His column proceeded through Enon Church and began spotting Union troopers a mile beyond, near Haw's Shop. A brief skirmish netted a few prisoners from the *5th United States Cavalry*, of which Fitz Lee had formerly been a lieutenant. He even remembered a few of his erstwhile friends who were still with the regiment! From them Stuart learned that the entire regiment was on the road ahead.

Stuart crossed Totopotomoy Creek cautiously and headed for Old Church, which he suspected would be garrisoned as an important crossroads used by Union wagons advancing up the Mechanicsville Turnpike. His suspicion was correct. There was only one good approach to the crossroads, straight up the road, so Stuart boldly sent his troopers charging. They slashed through the thin Union line and captured a number of prisoners along with five guidons and the deserted enemy camp.

Stuart had now accomplished the primary objective of his expedition. There were no Union lines south of Totopotomoy Creek, and he needed to get that information to Lee as soon as possible. But how should he return? The direct road to Richmond, the Mechanicsville Turnpike, led directly by the Union lines along the Chickahominy, and the Yankees were sure to be looking for him along the route he already covered. To be certain, Stuart probably could have dodged his way back to his lines by heading west towards the line of the Virginia Central Railroad. But the spirit of adventure had seized him. He felt that he had a good opportunity to strike at the Union supply line, the Richmond and York River Railroad, and perhaps stall McClellan's advance by tearing up a section of the tracks. His return to Lee's lines could then be made by riding south to cross the Chickahominy at Forge Bridge (which reports said to be damaged but repairable), and then heading back west around the Union left after making a complete circuit of McClellan's army. It was a bold, audacious plan, clearly beyond the instructions Lee had given, yet something Stuart may have wanted to attempt from the beginning of the expedition.

Stuart called together his colonels and decided to continue the raid rather than turn back as the officers urged. He called forward guides who were familiar with the ground to be covered and headed the column southeast towards Tunstall's Station. As they neared their goal, they saw some overturned wagons and clear evidence that the enemy knew they were near and so had fled for safety. Stuart pressed on eagerly. His impetuosity was rewarded when he saw two companies of Union infantry, the only guard at Tunstall's, formed up to face him.

The Yankees were no match for a determined cavalry charge and were easily scattered. Stuart ordered the telegraph lines to be cut, and his men set to work ripping up track. They had barely started when a Union train came up pulling flatcars full of soldiers. Stuart hastily tried to organize an ambush, but some ever eager trooper fired a shot that alerted the engineer, and the train sped off to safety.

Stuart was sorely tempted to push on to McClellan's supply base at White House, but at sunset he thought better of the idea. He gathered up some captured mules, set all the wagons afire that he could, and headed south towards St. Peter's Church. There was a full moon to light the way, but a bad road and the growing weariness of the troopers caused the column to stretch inordinately; it was midnight before the exhausted artillery battery reached Talleysville, four miles south of Tunstall's. To speed up the march, Stuart or-

dered two prisoners to ride each available mule. He had to reach the Chickahominy by dawn.

The troopers nodded in their saddles. Even the usually indefatigable Stuart gave in to his drowsiness, and one of his aides had to keep alert to prevent the general from falling off of his horse. At dawn Stuart tried to save time by fording the Chickahominy where he first met it, but he wasted two precious hours trying to cross the swollen torrent. He moved his command downstream a mile to Forge Bridge, and after much effort rebuilt the broken span using heavy timbers from a nearby warehouse. Fortunately, no Yankees appeared until the bridge was made useable and the happy troops had crossed. Stuart ordered the bridge to be set on fire, and the worst of the journey was over.

Stuart's exhausted command still had 35 miles to cover. At least there was little likelihood now of Union interference, as the Yankees had few cavalrymen on the south side of the river. In fact, Union efforts to intercept Stuart on the north side of the Chickahominy—movements directed by none other than Stuart's father-in-law, Brigadier General Philip St. George Cooke—had been totally ineffective. An elated Stuart rode on ahead of his men to Charles City Court House, then to Malvern Hill and the New Market Road to Richmond. He reached Lee on the morning of 15 June, 48 hours after the had embarked on the raid from Taylorsville.

Stuart was instantly hailed as a

hero, and he had indeed carried out a magnificent feat. The most important outcome of his foray was the information Lee needed to complete his plans to attack the Union right. Some historians believe that Stuart's ride may have harmed the Confederate cause by making McClellan more aware of a need to switch his supply base from the York River to the James River. This, though, does not appear to have been the case McClellan dismissed Stuart's ride as a sideshow and continued his plans to advance directly against the Confederate capital.

Stuart basked in the glory of his success, for which he was promoted to major general. He continued to do a superb job of scouting and carrying out other routine duties, but what he really yearned for was still more glory—glory he sought from a ride around McClellan's army in Maryland that fall and from a more spectacular ride around the Union army at the height of the Gettysburg campaign. The latter raid was definitely controversial as it contributed significantly to Lee's defeat in Pennsylvania in the summer of 1863.

Jeb Stuart led Lee's cavalry until he was mortally wounded at Yellow Tavern, near Richmond, while attempting to repel a Union cavalry raid on 11 May 1864. He was hit by a shot fired from a range of less than 15 yards by a .44 calibre cavalry pistol wielded by Private John A. Huff of Company E, *5th Michigan Cavalry*. Stuart died at 1938 the next day; Huff was killed in action 17 days later at Haw's Shop.

What's in a Name

Many Civil War battles are known by more than one name. Often the Confederates would call a battle by the name of the closest town, while the Federals would prefer to name the fight after a nearby river or stream. Most of the battles of the Peninsula campaign also go by various names, but for different reasons. Fighting was so spread out during a number of engagements that different units would call the engagement by the closest landmark, so creating several names for the same action. It is interesting to note that Johnston's last battle is known to the Confederates as Seven Pines because that is where they enjoyed their greatest success in the action, while the Federals call the same engagement Fair Oaks for that was where they were more victorious. Only one of the Seven Days Battles was named after a town by the Confederates (Mechanicsville) and a creek by the Yankees (Beaver Dam Creek).

DATE	BATTLE	ALTERNATE NAMES
31 May - 1 June	Seven Pines	Fair Oaks
25 June	Oak Grove	King's School House
		French's Field
		The Orchard
26 June	Mechanicsville	Beaver Dam Creek
27 June	Gaines' Mill	Cold Harbor
		Chickahominy
27 June	Garnett's Farm	Golding's Farm
28 June	Golding's Farm	Garnett's Farm
29 June	Allen's Farm	Peach Orchard
29 June	Savage Station	
30 June	Frayser's Farm	Glendale
		Nelson's Farm
		Charles City Cross Roads
		New Market Cross Road
		Willis Church
		White Oak Swamp
		Turkey Bend
30 June	Malvern Hill	Turkey Bridge
1 July	Malvern Hill	Crew's Farm
		Poindexter's Farm

CHAPTER IX

Mechanicsville

Confederate army commander General Robert E. Lee used the information gleaned from cavalry commander Jeb Stuart's ride around the Union army on 12-15 June to complete his plans to attack McClellan's lines on the north side of the Chickahominy. On Monday, 23 June, he met with his key generals at his headquarters on the Nine Mile Road outside of Richmond in order to explain his strategy. Present at the meeting were division commanders James Longstreet, A.P. Hill and D.H. Hill—and army commander Thomas J. "Stonewall" Jackson, who had just spent 14 hours in the saddle on the last leg of his journey from the Shenandoah Valley to Richmond. The meaning of Jackson's presence was at once clear to the division commanders—that he was bringing his army from the Valley to strike the right or rear of McClellan's army. The only question was where and when.

Lee first gave the outline and purpose of the attack. Jackson was to strike McClellan's right and drive it back, in the process clearing the bridges over the Chickahominy so that more troops might safely cross to the north bank. The army would then strike at McClellan's supply line, the Richmond and York River Railroad, in order to break up his ability to advance or start a siege. Confederate success in the operation would force McClellan's left wing to withdrew or come out of its prepared lines and fight.

The details of the attack were to proceed as follows. Jackson was to move his command to Hanover Court House and then to Ashland. When he reached Ashland he would send a message to Branch's brigade of A.P. Hill's recently enlarged division, encamped near Halfsink on the upper Chickahominy. Branch would then cross the river, clear the northern approaches to Meadow Bridge, and serve as a liaison between Jackson and A.P. Hill. Jackson would continue his march and swing east on the road to Cold Harbor in order to get beyond the Union right flank. Meanwhile, A.P. Hill would cross the Chickahominy at Meadow Bridge and march to Mechanicsville, in the process clearing the way for D.H. Hill and Longstreet to cross on the Mechanicsville Bridge. D.H. Hill would march to support Jackson in an attack on the enemy's right flank while A.P. Hill and Longstreet confronted the strong Union position along Beaver Dam Creek.

Lee's plan was a sound one, though it would rely on four critical elements in order to succeed. First, Jackson would have to make his march secretly and quickly, so that the enemy would not be alerted to his coming. Second, Jackson would need to locate the exact position of the enemy's right, so that he could turn it or attack it beyond the line posted along Beaver Dam Creek, which was considered to be too strongly posted to be taken by direct frontal attack alone. Third, the crossings at Meadow and Mechanicsville Bridges needed to be secured promptly once the operation began in order to allow D.H. Hill and Longstreet to cross and give weight to the Confederate attack. Fourth, and most important, McClellan's army south of the river had to be held in check lest it make an attack on the greatly weakened Confederate lines in front of the capital. Lee had discussed this issue at length with a concerned President Davis, and he was confident that the 25,000 troops to be left on the south side of the river (Magruder's and Huger's commands) would be able to hold in check the greatly superior number of Union troops that would be facing them. Lee was relying greatly on all the fortifications his men had constructed during the previous three weeks. He also counted heavily on McClellan's deliberateness and his reluctance to take risks. Magruder had bluffed McClellan earlier in the campaign at Yorktown, and Lee counted on repeating the scenario at Richmond. If his plans failed and McClellan uncharacteristically did make an attack on Richmond while most of the Confederate divisions were north of the Chickahominy, Lee was certain that Magruder and the trenches would hold the Yankees off long enough for him to recall his troops to the south side of the river.

After explaining his plan, Lee took the unusual step of excusing himself from the meeting in order to allow his lieutenants to discuss the plan and work out a timetable for its execution. All supported the attack except D.H. Hill, who preferred to assault the enemy's left near Bottom's Bridge; he was afraid that a Confederate victory north of the Chickahominy would simply force McClellan to switch his base from White House to the James River near Malvern Hill (which in fact is what would happen). Hill, however, did not press his opinion because it was clear that Lee and the others were already determined to attack the enemy's right. The generals then turned to a discussion of the timing of the attack. Since the two Hills and Longstreet were already basically in position to move, everything depended on when Jackson could bring up his army from the Shenandoah Valley. Jackson declared that his command was already on the move and would be at Hanover Court House the next day; the battle could start in two days, on 25 June. When Longstreet pointed out that road conditions might slow Jackson down more than he expected, "Stonewall" agreed to allow himself another day to get into position. The generals reported to Lee that the battle would begin on 26 June and the conference adjourned at dark.

After the meeting, Jackson rode all night—his second straight in the saddle—and reached the head of his command about 10 miles west of Hanover Junction. He was not pleased to find his column strung out for miles. This was because the muddy roads had delayed the troops, particularly the wagons and artillery, and nobody appeared to be in charge of the column to keep it closed up. Jackson had not left control of the column to any of his generals but instead had entrusted it to an aide, Major Robert Dabney, who had promptly become incapacitated by an intestinal problem. For these reasons Jackson had to spend most of 24 June closing up and reorganizing his column of march. This meant that he would have a long hard march of about 25 miles on the 25th in order to be ready to move from his assigned jump off position east of Ashland at 0300 on 26 June.

Jackson's march did not proceed smoothly on the 25th. The roads were still muddy and many of the bridges were washed out. Since the command did not have a pioneer corps or sufficient axes, almost every stream posed an obstacle, and halts to build makeshift bridges became more and more frequent. By nightfall the muddy and tired troops had not even reached Ashland, and were still five or more miles short of their assigned goal. Jackson was testy and tired—he may have had no more than 10 hours of sleep in the previous four days—but he resolved to make up for lost time by having his troops on the road at 0230 on 26 June. He notified Lee that he was running slightly behind schedule but planned to catch up.

Jackson's lateness was not the only problem Lee's plan was facing. On 24 June Union scouts had taken in a deserter from Jackson's column who reported the disturbing news that "Stonewall" was moving to attack Porter's right north of the Chickahominy. This news greatly alarmed McClellan, who had been uncertain of Jackson's whereabouts and intentions for several days. He nevertheless continued with his plan to begin moving his army closer to Richmond south of the Chickahominy. Around 0900 on 25 June Heintzelman's corps, supported by a few troops from Sumner's and Keyes' corps, was ordered forward from Seven Pines to seize ground from which they could support a larger attack Franklin was scheduled to make the next day on the Confederate lines at Old Church. Heintzelman fought all day to seize his objectives in what would be the first engagement of the Seven Days' Battles. The fight was variously called Oak Grove, The Orchard, King's School House, or French's Field, and cost each side about 500 casualties.

McClellan received still more disturbing news on the afternoon of 25 June that the enemy was planning something big. General Porter sent a message that a fugitive slave had come into his lines from Richmond and reported that Jackson was going to strike the Union rear and Beauregard had just arrived in the capital with troops from the west. This convinced McClellan that Lee was going to attack with greatly superior numbers, though he was not totally certain where. He went to the north side of the Chickahominy to inspect Porter's lines, and ordered all his commanders to be on the alert and have their men ready to fight the next day.

Jackson's column was on the move long before dawn on 26 June in his effort to get back on schedule. Its march, however, was slowed by the need to deploy skirmishers to the front and a flank guard on the left. As a result, Jackson did not reach the Virginia Central Railroad, five miles southeast of Ashland, until 0900—six hours behind schedule. He notified Branch of his arrival, but Branch did not inform A.P. Hill. All the Confederates south of the river were by then in their pre-attack positions, ready to move out. Lee must have been relieved that all was quiet farther to the right in front of Magruder and Huger; he had been greatly concerned by Heintzelman's advance and the fighting at Oak Grove the day before.

After passing the Virginia Central Railroad, Jackson divided his force so that it could move up more rapidly along two separate roads. Jackson led the eastern column, while Dick Ewell took a road that would swing two miles to the west. Despite being far behind schedule, Jackson halted his column at noon to allow his men to eat and rest. At 1300 he linked up with Jeb Stuart and some of his cavalry, which had been sent to screen his advance. About 1500 he reached Totopotomoy Creek, where he drove off a small Union outpost.

147

The Yankees, however, burned the bridge there and it took Jackson an hour to repair it. His vanguard reached Hundley's Corner, a mile to the south, at about 1700 and reestablished contact with Ewell's column coming up from the west. Jackson was now confused as to what to do next. He was near the position ordered by Lee, albeit six or more hours late, and there was no sign of D.H. Hill's troops, which were to support him on the right. He had heard some artillery fire to the south but was uncertain of its meaning. Instead of pushing on, he let his tired men go into camp. His singular lack of initiative can be explained today only by his own extreme weariness. Had he advanced, he would have been in Porter's rear and probably would have changed the course of the campaign.

The troops in Longstreet's, A.P. Hill's and D.H. Hill's divisions waited impatiently all day for their call to action. They had been in their jump off positions since early in the day, and grew restless and thirsty as the hot sun passed midday. Most impatient of all was Major General A.P. Hill. He had awakened his troops at 0200 and massed them in a woods south of Meadow Bridge, ready to march the instant he heard from Branch that Jackson was moving into position. As hour after hour passed and no messenger came from Branch, Hill, who was high-strung anyway, became so anxious that he could not stand it any longer. At about 1500 he took it on his own initiative to order an advance. It is not clear today why he did not consult with Lee, who was only two miles away. It was to be the third great Confederate error of the day, following Jackson's early bivouac and Branch's failure to communicate with A.P. Hill after he established contact with Jackson.

The men of Field's Virginia brigade, elated after their long hours of waiting, charged across Meadow Bridge and scattered the few Yankee pickets that were posted there. Field continued up the road to Mechanicsville, one and one-half miles distant, until he ran into Federal artillery fire from the village that stopped his advance cold. Hill brought up Pegram's six gun battery to support Field only to have the brave

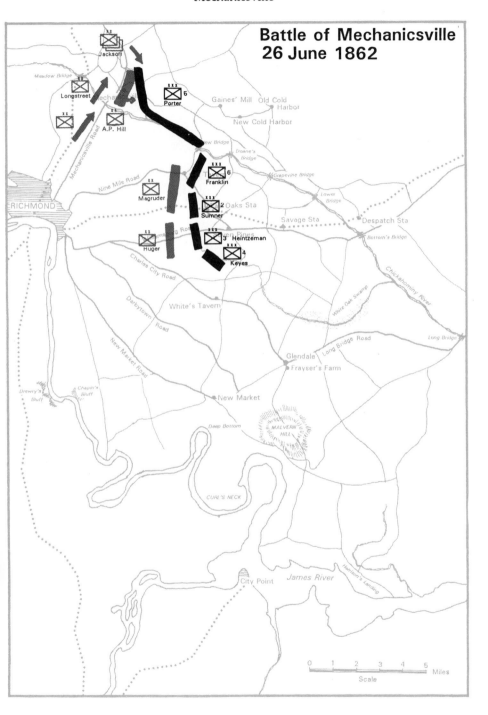

**Battle of Mechanicsville
26 June 1862**

Union guns located at Mechanicsville shell Confederate positions south of the Chickahominy River.

unit blasted by thirty Federal pieces—four of its guns were disabled and half of its men and horses fell casualty in just a few minutes. It was not an auspicious start to the battle.

Field stayed in position while Hill brought up the rest of his brigades. Their arrival caused the Yankee artillery, which had only been an outpost, to withdraw behind the main Union line one-half mile to the east. Hill was thrilled to seize Mechanicsville, and formed up his troops to begin an assault on the main Federal position. He then waited for Longstreet and D.H. Hill to come up as he strained to hear the sounds of Jackson's guns.

When Longstreet and D.H. Hill saw A.P. Hill's men in Mechanicsville about 1600, they began crossing the river according to Lee's plan. Part of the column, though, was delayed at least half an hour because of bridge repairs. Lee saw the movement from his headquarters and assumed that A.P. Hill was advancing because he had finally heard from Jackson. He started forward, but stopped to oversee the completion of the bridge repairs. As a result, he did not reach

BATTLE OF BEAVER DAM CREEK

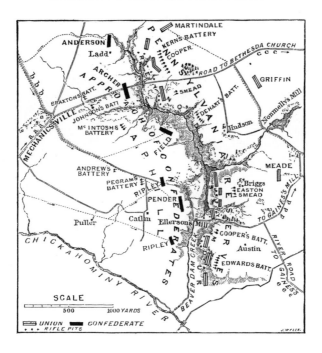

Mechanicsville until after 1700. He did not like what he learned there—that A.P. Hill had not heard from Jackson but had advanced on his own initiative. This put Lee in quite a quandary. He would soon have half of his army at Mechanicsville in front of a position he had no intention of assaulting head on. The Union line was very strongly posted on the hills behind Beaver Dam Creek, and the creek bed itself was a formidable obstacle, complete with stretches of quicksand. Yet, a battle seemed thrust upon him when some of A.P. Hill's troops, unable to withstand the Federal artillery fire in the open ground east of Mechanicsville, advanced to the woods nearer the creek for cover and began engaging the Union infantry in their front.

Lee was pressed to make an instant decision whether to disengage or mount a full attack. He boldly chose to attack, in hopes that Jackson would soon come up or would hear Lee's

The line of Porter's V Corps shudders under Lee's constant attacks during the battle of Gaines' Mill on 27 June. The constant pressure eventually forced the Federals to retreat.

Federal cannon pound advancing Confederate ranks during Gaines' Mill. Though Lee won the day there, his attack was confused, his casualties outweighed those of the enemy and the Yankees managed to escape in order.

guns and join the battle. A.P. Hill had already been massing his troops to the left of Mechanicsville, and about 1,800 moved forward with Anderson's, Archer's and Field's brigades. One Union soldier was amazed as the Confederates rushed forward "from the woods, out of the swamps, down the roads, along the entire front, with shriek and yell, flashing fire, thunder, and curling smoke." The attacking lines were shredded first by Union artillery, then by massed musketry. The Confederate infantrymen dodged for cover, then charged again. None made it to within a hundred yards of the Union position. The fighting raged on, and one regiment, the 35th Georgia, at last crossed the stream and pierced the enemy lines. But no supports came up, and what was left of the unit had to withdraw after suffering devastating losses. Hill's entire attack was repulsed in less than 30 minutes.

This should have been enough, but there would be one more bloody and fruitless Confederate assault. Late in the day A.P. Hill thought that the Federals might have weakened their left in order to meet his earlier attack on their right, so he sent two brigades (Pender's of his own division and Ripley's from D.H. Hill's) in an attack towards Ellerson's Mill, located just north of the Cold Harbor Road. The attack was launched at dusk and never had a chance. Pender's brigade advanced under heavy artillery fire and then attempted to charge; no one made it as far as the creek. The 38th North Carolina lost 152 of its 420 men in the attack, but it was not nearly as hard hit as the 44th Georgia, the only unit of Ripley's brigade to press the attack. That brave regiment charged straight at a Federal battery and was literally mowed down at the range of 70 yards, losing 335 of its 514 men. Darkness then saw a merciful conclusion to the infantry fighting, though the artillery of both sides continued to exchange fire for another three hours. The battle had cost Lee about 1,400 men for absolutely no gain. Porter reported his losses at only 361, all from McCall's division, his only unit engaged on the Beaver Dam Creek line.

CHAPTER X

Gaines' Mill

*U*nion Major General George B. McClellan witnessed the closing stages of the battle of Mechanicsville on the evening of 26 June and was elated at his troops' easy victory. Nonetheless, he was gravely concerned about the large enemy force lurking to the right of McCall's rear. After conferring with Porter until after midnight, he ordered him to withdraw his corps about four miles to a less vulnerable position behind Boatswain's Creek, near Gaines' Mill. Porter's 30,000 men were more than enough to cover the two mile long line that arced back from the Chickahominy to Old Cold Harbor and guarded the bridges on the Chickahominy in the rear of Sumner's corps. Porter formed his two fresh divisions in front (Morell's on the left, Sykes' on the right) and put McCall's now battle-hardened command in the rear. He left a strong rear guard behind that began a two hour artillery barrage near dawn on 27 June to discourage Confederate pursuit.

Lee was concerned about the firing the erupted from the Union lines, and set about organizing a flank movement to drive the Federals away from Beaver Dam Creek. Before the maneuver was started, the Union firing ceased. A.P. Hill sent Gregg's South Carolina brigade, his only fresh unit, forward to reconnoiter. Gregg rebuilt a bridge at Ellerson's Mill and cautiously moved forward past the scene of the previous day's carnage; at one point three dead Confederates were seen standing upright in the mud. Supported now by the rest of A.P. Hill's division, Gregg continued on to the east in pursuit of the Federals. Near Walnut Grove Church, about two miles from Ellerson's Mill, two men of Hill's advance guard were wounded by a column approaching from the left. Before battle could be joined, Hill's troops were relieved to discover that they had bumped into Jackson's division, which had finally started marching south from Hundley's Corner after a somewhat leisurely breakfast.

A short while later A.P. Hill and Jackson met at Walnut Grove Church. What the two officers said to each other is not recorded, since neither would survive the war. Hill understandably might have been annoyed that Jackson had not come to his aid the previous afternoon. Lee came up after awhile and conferred with the two officers briefly before Hill left. Lee spoke further with Jackson to explain the day's plan. He did not have harsh words for his weary lieutenant—he seldom lost his temper with his subordinates—but instead simply directed Jackson to hurry his march to Cold Harbor. Lee suspected that Porter might form behind Powhite Creek, near Gaines' Mill. If he did, Jackson would be able to strike the Union line from the rear; if not, Jackson could help A.P. Hill and Longstreet pursue the Yankees towards the Chickahominy or the Richmond and York River Railroad, whichever way they went. Lastly, Lee reminded Jackson that D.H. Hill's division would be under "Stonewall's" command as originally planned.

The direct pursuit of the Federals was conducted by A.P. Hill, who advanced southeast along the Cold Harbor Road, and Longstreet, who followed a roughly parallel road one-half mile to the west. A march of about seven miles brought Hill at noon to Gaines' Mill, where he found an enemy force deployed behind Powhite Creek. He at once formed Gregg's brigade, which had been leading his advance, and sent it forward in what, in Hill's opinion, was "the handsomest charge in line I have seen during the war." Gregg easily scattered the Union forces on his front and began chasing the retreating enemy over a crest and down towards a second creek. The Confederate advance, now slightly disorganized by their pursuit, was suddenly stopped in its tracks by a thunderous blast of Union artillery. Just then Lee and his staff rode up, and Lee moved forward to help rally Gregg's men. It was the first and not the last time that he would come under enemy fire during the war.

Gregg had found Porter's main line. It was not behind Powhite Creek as Lee expected, but was located in a stronger position behind the second stream, Boatswain's Creek, that was not even on Lee's map. Porter had selected this line for a number of good reasons. The channel of Boatswain's Creek was marshy, particularly on the right, and so formed much more of an obstacle than Powhite Creek. The creek itself flowed parallel to Powhite Creek for about a mile, and then bent east at almost a right angle to its sources over two miles away, south and east of Old Cold Harbor. This convex line enabled Porter to mass his firepower at the center and also to guard his right flank. Had he positioned his men along Powhite Creek, his right near Gaines' Mill would have been vulnerable to just the flanking move that Lee sent Jackson to accomplish. Porter's line behind Boatswain's Creek was now, by chance, in just the right position to block Jackson's advance on Old Cold Harbor. A final significant advantage of the Boatswain's Creek line was the fact that there was a large broad hill (Turkey Hill) that rose behind the creek that could not have formed a better site for a defense in depth. Porter posted most of his artillery on the crest of the hill, and was able to form two, sometimes three, lines of infantry on the lower slope of the hill between the guns and the creek. His defenses on this line were every bit as strong as the line he had been forced to abandon on Beaver Dam Creek, and were more heavily manned.

After rallying Gregg's brigade, Lee surveyed the Union lines and did not like what he saw. The only advantage the Confederates had was that Jackson was expected to fall on the enemy's rear at any moment. In order to distract Porter's

Battle of Gaines' Mill
27 June 1862

TACTICAL MAP OF THE BATTLE AT GAINES' MILL

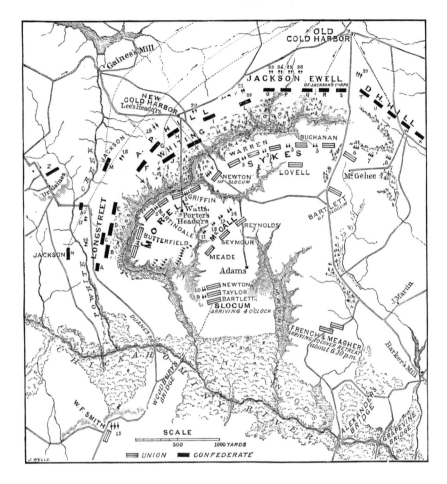

attention and prevent him from shifting troops to meet Jackson, Lee made the decision to order Hill to follow up Gregg's first attack. Hill received the order at about 1300 and within half an hour had most of his division formed in a three-quarter mile long line facing the enemy. He was concerned, however, about beginning the attack with no support on his left, where D.H. Hill was expected to come up, or on his right, where Longstreet was just beginning to arrive and deploy his men. A.P. Hill decided to wait for Longstreet to form. Longstreet's men, though, were in no hurry to begin the attack, and cautiously moved forward under heavy Federal artillery fire. As the minutes stretched into an hour and Longstreet was still not ready to attack, A.P. Hill decided that he could wait no longer and impetuously ordered his men forward, unsupported, for the second time in two days.

A.P. Hill ordered his batteries to open fire at about 1430. Their smoke soon covered the front with a heavy pallor that hung low because of the heat and humidity. He sent forward his four freshest brigades (Gregg's, Branch's, Anderson's and Archer's), none of which had been engaged the day before. The troops rushed forward with all the enthusiasm of young men in their prime who had never seen serious combat. They had to charge through open ground under artillery fire to reach the thickets near the creek and then cross the 60 foot wide marsh under heavy infantry fire. Still they came on, their bravery exciting the admiration of the enemy commander, General Porter: "Dashing across the intervening plains, floundering in the swamps, and struggling in the tangled brushwood, brigade after brigade seemed almost to melt away before the concentrated fire of our artillery and infantry; yet others pressed on, followed by supports as dashing and as brave as their predecessors."

The fighting was intensely fierce all along the line. On the left, Gregg's brigade ran into a heavy enemy cross fire but continued on. At some points it even managed to break into the Federal line. The men fought viciously with bayonets and clubbed muskets until driven back. One Confederate recalled, "There was no cheering. Every man was fighting with his mouth closed and standing his ground with all the courage he could command." In the center, Branch's North Carolinians had difficulty crossing the swampy creek, and no one made it to within a stone's throw of the Union lines. The firing here was so intense that the flag of the 7th North Carolina was struck by 32 bullets. Hill brought up Pender to Branch's support, but his men could do no better. Farther to the right,

Anderson made three charges without success. On the far right, Archer's brigade advanced by charging in 30 yard increments, with the men lying down between spurts. Their final charge was met by enemy fire that, as one Union soldier wrote, "mowed them down like grass."

The fighting went on for well over an hour, with Porter's men enjoying every advantage. As ammunition was depleted, new supplies were brought forward. Fresh regiments were rotated into the front lines to relieve those who became tired or started to take losses. McCall's Pennsylvania troops, who had at first been held in general reserve because they had fought the previous day, were brought forward to the areas of heaviest combat. One private from the *1st Pennsylvania Reserves* described his unit's advance to aid the *5th New York*: "When the fighting was severest, our regiment was ordered forward to reinforce the gallant zouaves; and as we advanced for that purpose, we could distinctly see the desperate nature of the fighting. Neither side appeared to think of loading their muskets, but depended entirely on the bayonet. We advanced as fast as possible to the assistance of the zouaves, but by the time we reached the ground the gallant fellows had beaten the rebels back into the woods and out of sight...The ground was so thickly covered with the dead and wounded that it was with the utmost difficulty we could advance without treading on them...The regiment was compelled to break ranks and get over the ground as best they could...A closer inspection of the field revealed the fact that the loss of the enemy was even greater. The nature of the wounds inflicted proved the close proximity in which the combatants contested for mastery. Some of the dead had their heads broken in by blows from butts of rifles, and others lay dead with bayonets thrust through them, the weapon having been left sticking in their bodies. Some of the wounded begged piteously to be helped to the rear; and altogether it was the most sickening sight I had ever witnessed."

Curiously, McClellan was at first unaware of the heavy

fighting, though his headquarters was only three miles to the south. Once again, atmospheric conditions were muffling the din of the battle, and all McClellan heard were some distant reports he took to mean that an artillery duel was in progress. He was preoccupied all day with Confederate activity in front of Richmond. There was sporadic skirmish fire all up and down the line, with occasional outbursts of artillery. Regiments were seen changing positions and moving in open view amidst a shouting of orders. At one point, a Confederate regiment, acting under mistaken orders, actually attacked the Union lines. All this activity persuaded the Federal troops, including McClellan, that Lee was going to conduct an all-out assault on their front at any moment. The true fact of the matter was that Magruder was putting on a "big show with a small number of troops," and in the process fooled McClellan into thinking that there were 100,000 Confederates in front of Richmond instead of one-fourth that number.

McClellan vacillated as to how best to deal with the situation. For awhile on 26 June he had considered using Porter's troops as bait for a trap to draw Lee's left wing farther from Richmond; he could then move with ease against the enemy line south of the Chickahominy and capture the enemy capital. Since such a move would necessitate the abandonment of his supply line on the north side of the Chickahominy and the base at White House, McClellan ordered his quartermaster to begin packing up his supplies for removal to a new base on the James River. Later on 26 June, however, McClellan began considering an alternative and opposite plan—to hold his left flank south of the river and move as much of his command as he could to Porter's support in order to defeat Lee in the more open ground north of the Chickahominy, where the Confederates would not have the advantage of prepared entrenchments. In preparation for this possible move, he ordered Franklin to have a division ready to cross immediately in support of Porter. He then began canvassing his corps commanders to determine how many troops they could spare to send north of the river. Sumner offered half of his men and Heintzelman offered one-third of his, while the cautious Keyes said he could spare none. Strangely, McClellan would spend all day on 27 June weighing his options, waiting for events to develop rather than attempting to take control of the situation. The only positive action he took all day was at 1400 when he finally directed Franklin to send Slocum's division to aid Porter. McClellan also suggested that Franklin send troops across the Chickahominy to strike the left flank of the Confederate forces at Gaines' Mill. Franklin replied that he could not do so because the only bridge in that sector had already been destroyed to keep it out of enemy hands.

Slocum's troops received their marching orders at 1430 and crossed the Chickahominy about 1500. They arrived on the north bank just in time to help Porter repulse the last of Hill's attacks. At about 1600 Hill directed his battered brigades to fall back. "These brave men have done all that any soldiers can do," he said later. "From having been the attacker I now became the attacked." His losses had indeed been tremendous, and with no gainful result. Gregg's South Carolina brigade had been particularly hard hit. The 1st Rifles lost 319 men, the 114th Regiment lost 208, and the 1st Regiment had 145 casualties.

For the second straight day A.P. Hill saw his command devastated as he waited for Jackson to come up behind the enemy's right. And he was not the only general waiting for Jackson to get into position that day. During the morning, D.H. Hill had marched across the front of Jackson's column as "Stonewall" was moving from Hundley's Corner towards Walnut Grove Church. Hill had been ordered by Lee to march to Cold Harbor and keep contact with Jackson's troops to his right. Hill headed northeast from Walnut Grove Church to Bethesda Church and then marched south to Old Cold Harbor, which he reached in the early afternoon. Advancing beyond the town, he unexpectedly ran into a line of Federals blocking his path. He had been expecting to strike the rear of the Union lines; instead he struck the right flank of Porter's line positioned behind Boatswain's Swamp. Sykes' division of U.S. Regulars, supported by at least 10 cannons, was more than Hill wanted to tackle alone, so he formed his men and waited for Jackson to come up.

Jackson was once again very late in arriving. Instead of following D.H. Hill's column after his morning conference with Lee at Walnut Grove Church, he had taken a different route under the direction of a local guide. Apparently Jackson simply told the guide that he wished to go to Cold Harbor, and then let the guide lead the way. As the column marched southward in the early afternoon, Jackson heard firing in his front. He asked the guide where the firing was coming from, and he responded that it came from the direction of Gaines' Mill. Jackson then asked if the road they were on went to Gaines' Mill, and the guide answered that it ran through Gaines' Mill to Cold Harbor. Jackson, clearly annoyed, said, "But I do not wish to go to Gaines' Mill; I wish to go to Cold Harbor, leaving that place on the right." To which the guide replied, "Then the left-hand road [the route that D.H. Hill had taken via Bethesda Church] was the one which should have been taken, and had you let me know what you desired, I could have directed you aright first."

There had clearly been an unfortunate misunderstanding, caused largely by Jackson's error at not being more explicit in his instructions to the guide. The guide was also partly at fault for not explaining to Jackson that there was an alternate route to Cold Harbor; he simply took the shorter and more direct way with no comment. There is also the possibility that the guide was taking Jackson to New Cold Harbor (located one-half mile east of Gaines' Mill instead of Old Cold Harbor) since Jackson had stated his goal to be simply "Cold Harbor." He probably was not aware that there were two villages of the same name, since he was not at all familiar with the area. One of his men later admitted, "The Chickahominy is not much like the royal Valley of Virginia, and we always felt lost on it."

Jackson needed only to march on another mile and he would have come into a good position between D.H. Hill's division, which was then nearing Old Cold Harbor, and A.P. Hill's command, which was soon to become embattled south of Gaines' Mill. Why he did not do so, or attempt to reach Old Cold Harbor by marching through New Cold Harbor, remains one of the great mysteries of this still confusing battle. Granted, he was probably not aware of A.P. Hill's or Porter's positions, but all he had to do was to send some scouts forward to investigate the firing he had heard to the south. He may have been more concerned that such a move would not have been in compliance with Lee's orders to attack the Union rear at Cold Harbor, not their front. In his official battle report (which was not filed until 20 February 1863), Jackson stated, "The enemy having obstructed the road which I had taken, and adopted the additional precaution to delay my march by defending the obstructions with sharpshooters, it became necessary, for the purpose of saving time, to take a road still farther to the left." It is interesting that no one else mentioned the barricades or Union sharpshooters in their reports. We can only wonder today why Jackson did not lay the blame on the guide or admit that he had taken the wrong road. Our best conclusion would be that he was confused about what was happening at the time and never did come to understand what went wrong during the march, or why.

Whatever were his reasons, Jackson ordered his troops to turn around and backtrack to the road that D.H. Hill had used earlier in the day. This route via Bethesda Church required him to march another three or four miles to get to Old Cold Harbor. The backtracking extended his march, and the difficulty in reversing his columns caused even greater delay in reaching his assigned position, much to the confusion of D.H. Hill on his left and A.P. Hill on his right.

As Jackson's column began retracing its steps, Major Walter H. Taylor of Lee's staff rode up, desperately seeking troops to support A.P. Hill's floundering attack. He found Dick Ewell, one of Jackson's division commanders, and urged him to leave the column and march to the southwest. Ewell did not feel that he had time to consult Jackson, whose whereabouts he did not know at the moment, and began following Taylor's lead back towards Gaines' Mill.

It is not known when Jackson learned of Ewell's departure from his column. As Ewell marched to the south and the rest of Jackson's command backtracked on their way to Old Cold Harbor, Jackson rode on ahead and reached D.H. Hill's waiting troops. Hill at the time was engaged in some heavy skirmishing with the opposing troops of Colonel Robert Buchanan's brigade of U.S. Regulars, which formed the far right of Porter's line. These troops did not enjoy any benefit from Boatswain's Swamp, which petered out on their left, but were protected instead by felled trees and a goodly supply of artillery. As Jackson came up, the Union guns were driving off Bondurant's Alabama battery, the only artillery Hill had in position, and were spraying the Confederate infantry with shells.

Jackson directed Hill to break off the engagement for the moment and withdraw to a more sheltered position. He then sent his quartermaster, Major John Harman, to order Brigadier Generals W.H.C. Whiting and Charles Winder to bring their divisions up and form on Hill's right, facing Boatswain's Swamp. Whiting, whose unit was in advance of Winder's, did not know Harman and refused to obey what he thought were unclear directions. The Confederate brigadier was a crusty individual who had only recently joined Jackson's command. He had already given Jackson trouble during the day, especially when his men by mistake started to fire at the rear of D.H. Hill's lines. Whiting refused to move for at least half an hour until Major Robert L. Dabney, another member of Jackson's staff, went on his initiative to see what was delaying the movement. Dabney was clearly more forceful or more persuasive than Harman, and finally succeeded at urging Winder to start moving into position on the right. Dabney's action was significant because Whiting's refusal to move had stalled Winder's large division that was behind him on the road. Why Jackson did not send someone or go himself to see what was delaying Whiting, is yet another enigma of the battle. He may have been preoccupied with getting D.H. Hill's troops into a protected position and with trying to bring up his artillery, which had been delayed by all the countermarching. One historian suggests that Jackson may have been waiting for the enemy to withdraw under pressure from Longstreet and A.P. Hill.

While Jackson's wing was stalled on the left, Dick Ewell was leading his division into action in the Confederate center. During mid-afternoon Ewell had left Jackson's column and proceeded through New Cold Harbor in an effort to support the left wing of A.P. Hill's division. He arrived at the front line soon after 1600, not long after Hill's men had pulled back from their long and unsuccessful attacks. Hill's troops were glad to see reinforcements come up since they were fearing a Union counterattack, and they tried to warn Ewell's men of the strength of the enemy lines. Brigadier General Isaac Trimble yelled back at them, "Get out of the way, we will show you how to do it!", before leading his men directly against the strongest part of the Union line.

Trimble's brigade, spearheaded by the 15th Alabama, led Ewell's attack, supported by Elzey's brigade on the left and by the Louisiana Brigade on the right. The charging lines endured heavy enemy fire as they crossed the swamp and started up the opposite hillside. Casualties were dreadful. Brigadier General Arnold Elzey received a terrible wound in the face, and Colonel Isaac Seymour, commander of the Louisiana Brigade, fell dead along with scores of his men. Burly Major Roberdeau Wheat, the 250 pound, six-foot four-inch commander of the famed Louisiana Tigers, fell pierced by numerous bullets about 20 paces from the Union line. For the first time in its career the Louisiana Brigade, hero of several battles in Jackson's Valley campaign, broke and ran. It had lost almost 300 men in just a few minutes. Its place in line was partially filled by Trimble's 21st Georgia as the battle raged on. For the first time in the day some Confederate troops were able to pierce the Union lines and maintain their position against fierce counterattacks. Ewell's two brigades, though, needed help, and were lucky to receive it in the form of Lawton's fresh Georgia command of 3500 men, the largest brigade in the army. General Ewell was so glad to see them that he shouted "Hurrah for Georgia!" as he brought it into line.

Farther to the right, Longstreet's division was at last entering the fray. Longstreet had brought his men up earlier in the afternoon and had taken the far right of the Confederate line. Due to an hour's delay cause by the need to repair broken bridges over Beaver Dam Creek, Longstreet had not come forward as fast as A.P. Hill's division which had come directly forward by road from Mechanicsville. This meant that Hill had his troops ready to attack long before Longstreet, who seemed to Hill to be dragging his feet at getting into position. As a result, the impetuous Hill had begun his attack at 1430 without any supports, as already discussed. As Longstreet brought his men up on the Confederate far right, he placed three brigades (Wilcox's, Pryor's and Featherston's) under the command of Brigadier General Cadmus Wilcox in the front line facing the Union troops on the other side of Boatswain's Creek. Pickett's brigade, which arrived next, was put in close reserve, while Longstreet's two other brigades (Anderson's and Kemper's) were still on the road.

Longstreet had wanted to attack as soon as his lines were formed but by then it was clear that Hill's assaults were not making progress against the strongly posted Union lines. Though Hill was clamoring for support, Lee directed Longstreet to hold his men back and await Jackson's expected attack on the Union right. Longstreet's lines held their position for two hours under enemy artillery fire until Longstreet received orders about 1630 to engage the enemy's front in support of Ewell's attack on their center. Longstreet sent Wilcox's three brigades forward at once. They easily drove back the Union skirmishers, but after crossing a deep ravine ran into intense artillery and musketry fire. Longstreet tried to assist the stalled advance by committing Pickett on Wilcox's left. Pickett ran into such heavy fire that his men had to throw themselves to the ground behind a small rise about 75 feet in front of the Union lines. When Pickett went forward to personally urge his men to renew their attack, he fell wounded. After awhile Longstreet saw that his attack was stalled and recalled his men with instructions "to engage steadily, only threatening assault." Thus the combat continued on this flank, but at reduced intensity.

While Longstreet was engaging the Union left and Ewell was assaulting their center, Jackson at about 1630 at last sent D.H. Hill forward against the Federal right. Hill's men did not make an orderly movement as his regiments were thrown into confusion by the swamp and became intermingled. Hill himself admitted that there was "a lapping of brigades and the separation of regiments from their proper places." In addition, Hill's left brigades under Garland, Anderson and Rodes hit the Union lines at such an angle that his right brigades under Colquitt and Ripley were not able to enter the fight. Hill's jumbled lines advanced until they ran into a hail of canister from several Union batteries posted near the McGehee House. The Confederates made disjointed attacks for more than an hour without success, yet continued to keep up their efforts.

After putting Hill's troops into action, Jackson about 1700 began riding down the Old Cold Harbor Road towards New Cold Harbor, sucking on a lemon as was his peculiar habit. He eventually ran into General Lee, who greeted him, "Ah General, I am very glad to see you. I had hoped to see you before." The words seem friendly enough, but for the mild mannered Lee they constituted quite a rebuke. Jackson did not make a reply. Lee continued to speak, gesturing towards Ewell's ongoing attack against the Union center. "That fire is very heavy, do you think your men can stand it?" To which Jackson promptly asserted, "They can stand anything. They can stand that."

Instead of giving Jackson the scolding he may well have deserved, Lee outlined to him the army's position. Ewell, supported by Lawton, was attacking the Union center, and Longstreet was engaging their left. As soon as Jackson had his troops in position between Ewell and D.H. Hill's division on the far left, the entire Confederate army would move forward in one grand assault to carry the Federal lines.

Lee's plan was direct enough, but it would require time to bring his remaining troops up into position. All the men of Jackson's command were still not formed, and "Stonewall" continued to be concerned about bringing up enough artillery. Lee's greatest concern was with his center, where A.P. Hill's troops were effectively out of action due to their heavier losses earlier in the day and at Mechanicsville the day before. Lee directed Jackson to send two brigades from his division (Fulkerson's and Cunningham's) to support A.P. Hill's right, and Whiting's two brigades were to be brought up on Ewell's right.

While the Confederates were forming for their final attack, Porter brought up the last of his reserves. He initially had posted Morell's division on his left and Sykes' division on the right. The first round of Confederate attacks had forced him to commit his remaining troops, McCall's somewhat bloodied Pennsylvanians. Reynolds' and Seymour's brigades had reinforced his center, while Meade's brigade was used to stiffen the right. When Slocum's division of Franklin's corps began arriving about 1530, its brigades were at once committed to buttress the front lines, with Newton and Taylor being sent to the center and Bartlett being assigned first to the left and then to the right. These reinforcements gave Porter a total of about 30,000 troops to face Lee's force of over twice that number. Porter had held on thus far because of the natural strength of his position and the disjointedness of the Confederate attacks. However, his men were beginning to weary from two days of fighting, and he did not know how much longer he could hold on without substantial reinforcements. He had appealed for more help, but McClellan was still indecisive and released only two additional brigades, Meagher's and French's of Sumner's corps, for service north of the Chickahominy.

The first Confederate troops to attack as a result of Lee's 1700 conference with Jackson were three of Longstreet's brigades. Sometime before 1800 Longstreet received Lee's attack order and was impressed by its urgency: "All other efforts had failed, and unless I could do something, the day was lost." Since his front line, composed of Wilcox's, Pryor's and Featherston's brigades, had already been engaged for well over an hour, Longstreet formed up Pickett's, Kemper's and Anderson's brigades for the attack. As they began to move forward at about 1830, an ominous silence descended on this and other parts of the battlefield, a calm before the coming storm.

Longstreet's brigades advanced at 1830 under heavy enemy fire, but managed to make some headway, particularly on the left, where Pickett's men began to make a dent in the enemy line. Pursuant to Lee's orders, the attack spread down the Confederate line as Ewell renewed his efforts in the center and Winder advanced two brigades of Jackson's division into and across Boatswain's Swamp. On the far left, D.H. Hill also intensified his attacks. For the first time that day, after four hours of fighting, the Confederates were finally coordinating their assault instead of making piecemeal attacks.

The crisis of the battle arrived shortly before 1900, when Whiting released his two fine brigades, Hood's and Law's, to the attack. Whiting's men had been frustrated by their forced inaction at Seven Pines, and were anxious to meet the foe. They certainly had travelled a circuitous route that day in order to reach the front. They had been involved in Jackson's

171

A Federal artillery position during the final Confederate assault at Gaines' Mill which sealed Lee's first major victory of the war.

countermarch early in the afternoon, and then had rested near Old Cold Harbor while Whiting argued with Jackson's aides, Majors Harman and Dabney, about whether or not to advance. At length Whiting had moved forward, but he wandered too far to the right and found himself at Gaines' Mill in the rear of A.P. Hill's exhausted division. There he had met General Lee and received instructions to move still farther to the right to support A.P. Hill's right. Whiting complied, but was not encouraged by the condition of the troops he had come to support: "Men were leaving the field in every direction and in great disorder; two regiments, one from South Carolina and one from Louisiana, were actually marching back from the fire...Men were skulking from the front in a shameful manner; the woods on our left and rear were full of troops in safe cover, from which they never stirred."

Whiting's senior brigade commander, Brigadier General John Bell Hood, led his men into position with a special sense of purpose. As he came up, he found Lee sitting on his horse. Lee greeted him friendily and explained how the troops had been fighting gallantly but had not succeeded in dislodging the enemy. Lee continued, "This must be done. Can you break the line?" Hood replied that he would certainly try, and continued forward. Some accounts state that Lee added, "May God be with you" as Hood's men marched by.

While Hood was moving up, he received an appeal for help from Ewell and detached his 5th Texas and the Hampton (South Carolina) Legion to go to his aid. He then formed the 18th Georgia and 1st Texas on Law's right, with the 4th Texas in reserve. The command had to wait over an hour before orders came to advance in a charge that would be one of the greatest of the war. As his line surged forward, Hood noted an open field to the right of the 18th Georgia, about 800 yards in front of the enemy line. Hood related, "I therefore marched the Fourth Texas by the right flank into this open field, halted and dressed the line whilst under fire of the long range guns, and gave positive instructions that no man should fire until I gave the order; for I knew full well that if the men were allowed to fire, they would halt to load, break the alignment, and, very likely, never reach the breastworks."

Hood led the 4th Texas personally. The unit proceeded quickly across the open field and thus moved ahead of the rest of its brigade, which was slowed by woods and the swamp. "Onward we marched under a constantly increasing shower of shot and shell...Our ranks were thinned at almost every step forward, and proportionately to the growing storm of projectiles. Soon we attained the crest of the bald ridge within one hundred and fifty yards of the breastworks. Here was concentrated upon us, from batteries in front and flank, a fire of shell and canister, which ploughed through our ranks with deadly effect...At a quickened pace we continued to advance, without firing a shot, down the slope, over a body of our soldiers lying on the ground, to and across the creek, when, amid the fearful roar of musketry and artillery, I gave the order to fix bayonets and charge. With a ringing shout we dashed up the steep hill, through the abatis, and upon the very heads of the enemy."

As the Texans' piercing Confederate battle cry spread over the field, Hood halted the line 10 yards from the Union works and directed the men to open fire. Their tremendous volley ravaged the New Jersey troops in their front. Indeed, the speed of the 4th Texas' advance had caught the Yankees somewhat by surprise, especially since the heavy battle smoke limited visibility to only 20 yards. One New Jersey officer wrote, "The volley that fell upon our brigade was the most withering I ever saw delivered, for the men were totally unprepared for it. The New Jersey Brigade broke to pieces." The Yankees who fled from the first line overran and disorganized their second line. The 4th Texas pressed on, supported now by the rest of Whiting's division on the left and by Pickett's brigade on the right. The Confederate attack pealed back Union regiments on the right and left and headed for the strong line of Federal artillery posted on the hill behind the Watt house. The batteries blasted away with charges of double canister, tearing huge gaps in the Confederate lines. Hood's men bravely closed the gaps and pressed on to the very muzzles of the guns.

The situation was indeed critical, and there was no Union infantry at hand to help the gunners save their pieces. Brigadier General Philip St. George Cooke, McClellan's cavalry commander and the father-in-law of Confederate cavalry commander Jeb Stuart, was nearby with a squadron of the *5th United States Cavalry* and was not about to let Hood's men overrun the guns. He ordered the bugles to be sounded, and the blue clad cavalrymen went charging into the Texans in one of the few charges Union cavalry would make during the war against enemy infantry. One of the Texans later wrote that he "felt the ground begin to tremble like an earthquake and heard a noise like the rumbling of distant thunder." The valiant attack never had a chance. The Confederate infantry opened fire at 40 paces and emptied scores of saddles. All the horsemen who reached the contested cannons were shot or bayonetted. The survivors of the unfortunate squadron broke to the rear, leaving behind 156 of their 257 men as casualties. They also left Hood's men in possession of 14 of the 18 cannons they had boldly assaulted head on. The Texas Brigade had earned eternal glory for its attack but at the terrible cost of over 600 casualties, including 256 of 530 men in the 4th Texas and 145 in the 18th Georgia.

The strength and depth of the Confederate attack was too much for the outnumbered Yankees, many of whom had been fighting all afternoon. Cooke's retreating cavalrymen disordered additional troops that were trying to reform and all became chaos. One witness wrote that "The panic extended. Scores of gallant officers endeavored to rally and re-form the stragglers, but in vain, while many officers forgot the pride of their shoulder straps and the honor of their manhood...That scene was not to be forgotten: scores of riderless, terrified horses dashing in every direction; thick-flying bullets singing by, admonishing of danger; every minute a man struck down; wagons and ambulances and cannon blocking the way; wounded men limping and groaning and bleeding amid the throng; officers and civilians denouncing and reasoning and entreating, and being insensibly borne along with the mass; the sublime cannonading; the clouds of battle smoke, and the sun just disappearing, large and blood red." Amidst the confusion was the macabre scene of a splendid horse running crazed with a man's bloody left leg in its stirrup.

While the battle came to a climax on the Union left, the fighting had also intensified on the right. As already discussed, D.H. Hill had sent his troops into action about 1630 and had been unsuccessful at penetrating the Union lines because of intense artillery fire. About 1800, Hill met with two of his brigadiers, Garland and Anderson, who proposed to move against the enemy's right flank. Hill pointed out, however, that such a move would fall under flanking fire from one particular Union battery. Clearly, that battery had to be attacked and silenced. Garland said that he was willing to take the risk, and volunteered to send one of his regiments head on against the enemy guns. Hill promised to send two regiments in support of Garland's unit, while two more would be sent against the battery's flank. In addition, Hill pledged to send his whole division to follow up the attack after the battery was silenced.

Garland selected the 20th North Carolina, led by Colonel Alfred Iverson, to spearhead the attack on the battery. Iverson was supposed to be supported by the 1st and 3rd North Carolina regiments of Ripley's brigade, but these units never received the order and Iverson had to attack alone. In order to reach the Union lines the 20th North Carolina had to cross 400 yards of open ground under enemy fire. The precision of the Tarheels' advance won the admiration of their foes: "We witnessed as complete a move by the enemy as could be made on drill or parade. They came out of the woods at double-quick, with guns at right-shoulder shift, and by a move known to us as 'on the right by file into line' formed the line of battle complete. We had not long to admire them. Forward they came, intending to strike our line on the right. Not a gun did they fire until within less than fifty yards, when after a volley they gave a yell, and charged, five lines deep."

The brave Carolinians charged right up to a section (two guns) of Captain John Edwards' battery of the *3rd U.S. Artillery* and captured the pieces after a bloody hand-to-hand combat with its cannoneers. The Confederates held the guns for no more than 10 minutes before they were counterattacked by the *16th New York* of Slocum's division of Sumner's corps, which had been sent across the Chickahominy at 1500 to come to Porter's aid. The *16th New York*, part of Bartlett's brigade, had at first been assigned to Porter's left, but was then ordered to march to reinforce the far right. The brigade marched behind the Union lines all across the battlefield under heavy Confederate artillery fire that caused a number of casualties.

As soon as they reached the right, the men of the *16th*, wearing distinctive straw hats, rushed forward in a counter-attack to regain Edwards' lost guns. Bartlett helped lead the charge and admired his men for showing "the calmness and precision of veteran soldiers" in their first battle. After giving three cheers, the New Yorkers retook the cannons, but at a terrible cost—its colonel, Joseph Howland, was badly wounded, and 231 of its 510 men fell casualty, leaving their straw hats strewn everywhere on the bloody field. The 20th North Carolina likewise suffered heavily—its commander, Colonel Alfred Iverson, fell wounded early in the charge, and the regiment lost 272 men in the action, the second highest Confederate regimental loss in the battle.

The survivors of the *16th New York* held the recaptured cannons under heavy Confederate fire until they exhausted their ammunition and were forced to withdraw. They had been unable to remove the guns because they lacked horses, so the two cannons sat unattended, save by the dead and the dying, until the 5th Virginia of Winder's "Stonewall" Brigade came up to claim them later in the fight.

Meanwhile, the contest had become desperate for the Yankees on their right wing as well. Hill's promised flank attack at last hit home, putting the Union lines under a cross fire. One Union regiment after another broke or headed to the rear, so uncovering the flanks of neighboring units. The commander of the *10th U.S. Regulars* formed his command astride the Old Cold Harbor Road on a hill behind the McGehee House and held on until his command was swept away by a volunteer regiment that broke nearby. As the Union line collapsed, a few units valiantly stepped forward to try to stem or at least delay the Confederate advance. Among them was the *2nd U.S. Regulars*, which made a desperate charge to hold the enemy off long enough for another threatened battery to es-

A Union field hospital containing the dead and wounded from the defeat at Gaines' Mill. The Federals lost 6,837 men, many of them captured, but inflicted 8,751 casualties on their enemy.

cape. The battle raged around the McGehee House until past 2000, when darkness began to fall. Two regiments of Elzey's brigade finally managed to get into the woods behind the house, and all the U.S. Regulars who could not escape were captured. Some weary Union regiments formed a temporary line one-half mile southwest of the McGehee House and managed to hold on until Meagher's and French's fresh brigades came up from the river. These reinforcements marched forward with loud cries of "Huzzah!" that made some dispirited *V Corps* men believe that the Confederates had seized the Chickahominy River bridges in their rear.

As the victorious Confederates pressed forward, gathering in numerous prisoners and Union cannons, their units became hopelessly intermingled. D.H. Hill, senior officer on the far Confederate left, took charge of Winder's and Lawton's troops, who had helped break the Union right. He became concerned that the enemy might have heavy reinforcements near the river, so he called off the pursuit about 2100 and let his men bivouac in the captured Union lines. The move had Lawton's concurrence, but Winder strongly objected. Hill much later had to agree that "Winder was right; even a show of pressure must have been attended with great results." Firing continued on this front until after midnight as the battered Yankees withdrew across the Chickahominy. The troops on the Confederate right did not press their pursuit, either, being more exhausted and disorganized than those on the left.

The battle of Gaines' Mill was Lee's first great victory, but it was a most costly one. It had taken most of his army five hours of desperate fighting to overcome less than one-third of McClellan's army. Had Jackson advanced on time to strike Porter's rear and had A.P. Hill not attacked prematurely, the victory would have been more complete and less costly. Total Confederate losses among their 57,018 engaged were 8,751 killed and wounded. Only four brigade commanders were lost (Brigadier Generals George Pickett and Arnold Elzey were wounded and Colonels Isaac Elzey and S.V. Fulkerson were killed), but a large number of promising regimental officers were lost. Union casualties amounted to 6,837 (including 893 killed and 3,107 wounded) out of 34,214 engaged. They also lost 22 cannons and 2,836 men captured.

Among the Union captured was Brigadier General John F. Reynolds of the Pennsylvania Reserves. Reynolds was cut off when the Union right collapsed while he was posting a battery there near sunset. He apparently got lost in a swamp while trying to get to the rear after his horse was wounded. He then fell asleep from exhaustion, and was captured by Confederate pickets the next morning and taken to General

D.H. Hill. Hill and Reynolds had been friends during their pre-war service in the old army. This, and the circumstances of his capture, caused Reynolds great embarrassment. Hill later wrote, "General Reynolds seemed confused and mortified at his position. He sat down and covered his face with his hands, and at length said, 'Hill, we ought not to be enemies.' I told him that there was no bad feeling on my part, and that he ought not to fret at the fortunes of war, which were notoriously fickle." Reynolds was sent to Libby Prison in Richmond and remained there until he was exchanged on 13 August 1862. He rose to command the *I Corps*, and was killed in action at Gettysburg on 1 July 1863 while in command of the army's left wing.

CHAPTER XI

Savage Station

*U*nion army commander Major General George B. McClellan was greatly discouraged when he heard that Porter's corps had been pushed back all along its line near Gaines' Mill on the evening of 27 June. Throughout the day he had concentrated his attention on the apparent aggressiveness of the Confederate troops south of the Chickahominy so much that he only sent five brigades to aid Porter. When an encouraging message came from Porter at 1600 that he was holding his own, McClellan even suggested that he conduct a counterattack! For a time McClellan even pondered attacking Richmond or taking his whole army to fight a decisive battle north of the Chickahominy. All these options vanished with Porter's defeat. McClellan now had no choice but to withdraw all his troops to the south side of the river and complete the cautionary evacuation of his supply base at White House that he had begun the day before. He could establish a new base on the James River near Malvern Hill, but this would take time and would require the preparation of a new campaign strategy. When he wrote the day's bad news to Secretary of War Stanton late that night, he was demoralized and exhausted after sleeping less than 12 hours total in the previous three days. He blamed the day's defeat on the enemy's overwhelming strength, and promised, as usual, to win a victory if only he could receive more reinforcements.

It was well after dark when McClellan made his decision to retreat to the James. He announced it to his corps commanders at a meeting convened at 2300. The officers were subdued as they learned the degree of Porter's defeat and received their marching orders for the next two days. Keyes, whose *IV Corps* held the army's left and so was closest to the James, would move to secure the passages over White Oak Swamp. Porter's battered *V Corps* would follow as soon as it crossed the Chickahominy, and then would march to Malvern Hill in order to guard the army's trains as they moved to the James. Franklin's, Sumner's and Heintzelman's corps were to remain where they were for the moment in order to cover the withdrawal of the rest of the army. They would move to rejoin the other corps on 28 or 29 June, once the trains safely reached the James.

All of McClellan's corps commanders except Heintzelman accepted the necessity of the withdrawal to the James. As soon as the meeting was over, Heintzelman shared his opinions on the movement with his two aggressive division commanders, Brigadier Generals Phil Kearny and "Fighting Joe" Hooker. All agreed that the army should not retreat without a fight from its lines that were in sight of Richmond, a position it had taken over three months to reach. The trio rode to McClellan's headquarters and at the late hour of 0200 presented their arguments for not withdrawing the army. The fiery Kearny even advocated an immediate attack on Lee's weakened lines before Richmond. When McClellan refused to consider the option, Kearny urged that he at least be allowed to take a division and try to enter Richmond long enough to free the 14,000 Union prisoners being held there. McClellan refused this option also, at which point Kearny began such a verbal tirade that his comrades feared that McClellan might court-martial him.

McClellan's strategy was actually not as bad as the hotheaded Kearny argued. Though not aggressive or risky, the withdrawal to the James did offer a chance to regroup and still salvage the campaign. Lincoln wrote McClellan on 28 June with encouragement to save the army; the defeat, he said, was not McClellan's fault since the enemy had "ganged up" on him; reinforcements would be forthcoming so that McClellan could continue the campaign. The greatest problem posed by his withdrawal was the obstacle of White Oak Swamp, which was even more swollen than the Chickahominy and had only a limited number of crossings. McClellan's army would need almost two days to file across the swamp with all its wagons and cannons, and the army would be vulnerable to attack while it was strung out on the approaches to the swamp crossings. That is why McClellan chose to hold Sumner, Franklin and Heintzelman in position for a day or two in their prepared lines near Seven Pines. It is most curious, however, that McClellan did not pay more attention to guarding the Chickahominy in the rear of his army in order to prevent the Confederates from crossing should they try to build new bridges at any point.

28 June passed relatively quietly as Lee's troops south of the Chickahominy held their position, and those that were north of the river were unable to cross. The last of Porter's troops crossed to the south of the Chickahominy by 0400, and his engineers destroyed all the bridges. Throughout the day McClellan's most pressing problem was the evacuation of the huge quantities of supplies that he had stored up for his anticipated attack on the Confederate capital. He also had over 2,500 cattle to send south, as well as nearly 15,000 horses and mules that pulled some 3,000 wagons and ambulances, not to mention his siege train and over 100 cannons in his reserve artillery. It was not long before a massive traffic jam of troops and wagons developed on the swamp's causeways. McClellan knew that he could not withdraw all his accumulated supplies, so he ordered massive quantities to be burned. Huge columns of smoke would soon rise to the sky as provisions, ammunition and other impedimenta of war would be put to the torch. At least one fully loaded ammunition train would be sent plunging into the Chickahominy at the end of a burning trestle in a magnificent but bizarre spectacle.

There was also a huge amount of waste and destruction at the Union supply base at White House on the York River. After Porter's corps withdrew across the Chickahominy, there were only a few troops left to guard the base against Lee's imminent approach. Generals Stoneman and Casey saw to the evacuation of as many stores as could be transported by available ships. Everything that remained was set afire in a huge conflagration kindled on the evening of 28 June. A Union doctor who was present described the awesome scene: "The post office and quartermaster's tents, the officers' and sutlers' tents, the Negro quarters and railroad shanties, then the White House itself, were given to the flames. The flame, smoke and noise from the crackling and falling timbers made the scene one of the grandest imaginable, throwing a lurid glare for miles around and over the river in strange contrast with the sunlight. The light from the fire continued until after dark and lit up the heavens, making visible for miles the scene of the destruction. The White House itself, situated as it was on a high bluff, must have been seen blazing at a great distance. Many mourned its destruction, which, I learn, was contrary to the orders of General Casey."

Lee at first did not understand McClellan's movements on 28 June. After Porter's defeat at Gaines' Mill, Lee expected that McClellan would withdraw towards the Union supply base at White House; there also was a chance that the Yankees might withdraw up the Peninsula back to Fort Monroe. Porter's withdrawal to the south side of the Chickahominy caught Lee by surprise, with the result that he did not have his troops in position to pursue or attack McClellan on 28 June. Since McClellan's destruction of the bridges on the Chickahominy made it impossible for him to cross and attack the Union rear, Lee's only major movement on 28 June was to send Ewell's division to Despatch Station in order to block the Richmond and York River Railroad. He also sent a few batteries to the river to shell the flank and rear of Franklin's troops, who were still posted on McClellan's right immediately south of the Chickahominy and the battlefield of 27 June. Lee let the remainder of his troops that fought at Gaines' Mill have a much needed day of rest.

Lee now needed to locate the various parts of McClellan's command and to determine his foe's intentions. If McClellan were to concentrate his army immediately south of the river, Lee would be put in an awkward position and could not hold the ground that he had gained, especially if McDowell began to advance again from Fredericksburg. If Lee chose to try to cross the lower Chickahominy in order to attack McClellan's rear, there was the distinct danger that McClellan might attack Richmond's depleted defenses. Nor did Lee like the prospect of a Union movement along the James in the direction of Petersburg or Richmond's southern approaches.

Lee's understanding of McClellan's intentions became clearer late on 28 June after Ewell occupied Despatch Station and Stuart reported the findings of the patrols that he had sent out north of the Chickahominy. Stuart's men had witnessed the destruction of the Union supply base at White House, and reported that there were no large bodies of Federal troops still north of the river. This information, coupled with the fires seen burning behind Savage Station and reports of Union wagons moving towards the James, made it clear that McClellan was withdrawing from his advanced position near Richmond. Lee understood that it would be to his advantage to try to catch the Union army while it was on the move, and on the morning of 29 June he issued orders to carry out this objective. Jackson would rebuild the Grapevine Bridge and cross the Chickahominy with his own, Ewell's, Whiting's and D.H. Hill's divisions in order to strike the Union rear. Magruder would pursue the enemy straight up the Williamsburg Road. Meanwhile, Huger would advance up the Charles City Road to strike at the Union troops that were crossing White Oak Swamp. The hardest march would be made by Longstreet's and A.P. Hill's commands, which would recross the Chickahominy and march out along the Darbytown Road to hit the Union troops posted near the James River. Lastly, Holmes' division, which had just crossed from the south bank of the James, would march to cover the left flank of the troops on the Darbytown Road.

Lee's orders caused Magruder a great deal of anxiety. He had already been conducting demonstrations along his lines in front of Richmond for several days in order to pin down McClellan's forces south of the Chickahominy. These efforts included some artillery fire directed across the Chickahominy into Porter's rear during the battle of Gaines' Mill, and a probe on the evening of 27 June by two regiments of Toombs' brigade (2nd and 15th Georgia) that expanded into a two hour long engagement known as the action at Garnett's Farm. Lee's orders on 28 June directed Magruder to remain vigilant, ready to advance as soon as the enemy showed signs of withdrawing, yet he was not to attack unless directed by Lee or if the prospects of success seemed certain; Lee did not want Magruder to provoke McClellan into making a counterattack that might reveal the weakness of Magruder's line.

Magruder must have failed to relay these instructions to his subordinates, because late on the morning of 28 June he was astonished to find one of his division commanders, Brigadier General David R. Jones, preparing to attack the Union works on his front near Golding's farm. Jones had interpreted some Union troop movements to mean that the enemy was preparing to retreat, and he was anxious to mount a pursuit. After moving up some guns to shell the enemy, he had vainly attempted to locate Magruder. On his own initiative, he decided to direct his two brigadiers to attack if they thought that the Union line was weakened. Magruder, of course, was dumbfounded at Jones' brashness, and at once ordered him to retract his orders. But it was too late. G.T. Anderson had already ordered two of his regiments (7th and 8th Georgia) forward, and they had even managed to seize part of the Union outer lines. They were at once withdrawn, and the action at Golding's Farm came to an abrupt conclusion. The Yankees were clearly still maintaining their position in strength; the movements Jones had seen had only been a shifting of troops to the left to cover the withdrawal of Keyes' corps from the far left of the Union line.

The Union troops facing Magruder were actually pleased to hold their lines all day on 28 June as the army's trains and Keyes' and Porter's corps moved south; Magruder's probes, especially those at Garnett's Farm and Golding's Farm near the Chickahominy, had made them anxious about Confederate intentions. Early on 29 June, the three Union corps still in position near Richmond at last received word to start withdrawing. The troops began pulling out at 0300, leaving a small rear guard to hold their entrenchments as long as possible in order to deceive the enemy. Many of the Yankees were confused and disheartened by the retreat, since they had worked so hard to come so close to Richmond and had suffered no defeat to force them back. One surgeon wrote of the scene, "The men slung their knapsacks and quietly moved off. A scene of desolation met their view as they passed along. Tents cut to pieces, commissary stores thrown upon the ground or burning in heaps, blankets and clothing piled promiscuously about...all indicating a retreat under the most disastrous circumstances. Sumner withdrew his corps to Allen's Farm, one mile past Fair Oaks Station, where he let his men go briefly into bivouac as the army's rear guard; Heintzelman's and Sumner's troops continued on another two miles to Savage Station on the Richmond and York River Railroad.

General Magruder was not aware of the Union withdrawal from his front until shortly after dawn. The General was not at his best that morning, since he had not slept well because of indigestion caused by the strain of the previous four days. Right after he reported the enemy's departure to Lee, he received a messenger from his commander bearing news of the enemy's withdrawal; Longstreet's troops north of the Chickahominy had noticed the enemy movement long before Magruder's did! Lee even sent along a slightly sarcastic warning for Magruder to be careful when he advanced not to harm some of Longstreet's engineers who had already crossed the river. Shortly afterwards, Lee crossed to the south side of the river and personally gave Magruder orders to pursue and attack the enemy rear; Magruder would receive support from Jackson on his left and the rest of the army on his right.

Magruder formed his six brigades of 11,000 men astride the Richmond and York River Railroad near Fair Oaks Station and began a cautious advance, led by Kershaw's South Carolina brigade. Kershaw advanced over a mile from Fair Oaks and began to make contact with skirmishers of Sumner's command, still at Allen's Farm. As he advanced farther up the railroad line about 0900, Kershaw met even heavier fire and pulled his men back for fear he had run into Jackson's men coming in from the left. This fight, called the action at Allen's Farm, did not please Magruder, who suddenly became anxious about the lack of support on his right and the possibility of an enemy attack. He recalled Kershaw, though his skirmishers continued to spar with Sumner's, and sent messengers to Jackson and Lee for help. Jackson, he learned, was still north of the Chickahominy trying to repair the Grapevine Bridge, which would not be ready for another two hours. Lee was astonished at Magruder's sheepishness, since he understood the Yankees to be in full retreat. He sent a reassuring message to Magruder and promised to send two of Huger's brigades to his support. These troops, however, would have to be returned to Huger if they were not engaged by 1400.

Magruder waited until 1100 for Huger's men to come up on his right. Huger at last rode up ahead of his two brigades and was disappointed to see only a few Yankees in front of Magruder; Sumner had started pulling his troops back to Savage Station at 1100. Magruder tried to persuade Huger to bring his men up and join him in an attack on the Union position, but Huger decided that his presence was not needed. In accordance with instructions received from Lee, he turned his brigades back towards the Charles City Road.

Magruder was disheartened by Huger's departure, but pursuant to Lee's orders he now had no choice but to resume his advance. McLaws' troops had long since cleared the Union rear guard out of Allen's Farm, and Magruder began a slow pursuit of the enemy. It was already early afternoon, and the opportunity to deal the enemy the defeat that Lee had planned was fast disappearing. Sometime after 1500 Magruder located the Union lines drawn up west of Savage Station. He was uncertain how many troops he faced, and gingerly sent Kershaw's brigade to lead the advance on the Union position. Three brigades supported Kershaw, while two more under D.R. Jones were posted north of the railroad. Heavy undergrowth permitted only a few batteries to be brought into position on the right. Moral support was furnished by a large 32 pound rifled gun mounted on a flat car that was pushed up by an engine. It seemed like quite a contraption to one of Kershaw's soldiers, who wrote that the monster gun "gave out thundering evidences of its presence by shelling the woods in our front." The Federals responded with fireworks of their own as a huge supply dump near Savage Station was set afire, and bursting ammunition boxes and whiskey barrels sent debris flying into the sky.

It was not until after 1700 that Magruder's attack finally got under way. All the fighting occurred south of the railroad, as Jones on the left never received his attack orders. Kershaw's brigade led the way, and was stunned by a galling fire of musketry and artillery. His brigade had unknowingly struck not a small Union rear guard but Sumner's entire corps, supported by Smith's division of Franklin's corps. Kershaw's men charged on, becoming increasingly disorganized, until they met a blast of enemy grapeshot that sheered off a whole stand of young pine trees. August Dickert, author of a fine history of the brigade, went down with a bullet wound in the chest and soon received a second wound in the thigh from

A scene of the deterioration of McClellan's Peninsula campaign. Large amounts of Federal stores were set afire as troops prepared to retreat from Richmond.

friendly troops in the rear.

Semmes' brigade, which entered the action on Kershaw's right along with two Mississippi regiments of Barksdale's brigade, met similar stiff resistance. As the battle raged on, momentum shifted to the Union side. About an hour before sunset the *Vermont Brigade* of Smith's division made a counterattack on the south side of the Williamsburg Road that broke through two lines of Confederate infantry. The *5th Vermont* emerged from a woods into an open field right in front of Kemper's Virginia battery. The Confederate artillery pieces mowed the Vermonters down with grape and canister, while musketry cross fire increased their losses.

The bold regiment adjusted its line and held on while the men's guns became almost too hot to handle. Their bravery cost the unit 189 of its 428 men, the greatest battle loss of any

Yankees of the 16th New York, known for their conspicuous straw hats, join the retreat of the VI Corps during the predawn of 29 June. The darkness is lit by fired stores.

Vermont unit in the war.

Fortunately for the Confederates, a thunderstorm came up near sunset and brought a merciful end to their ill-conceived battle. They were also lucky that the Union defense was not organized well enough to mount a counterattack that would have caused serious difficulties for the Southerners. McClellan had gone to Harrison's Landing earlier in the day to supervise the setting up of a new supply base on the James, and had neglected to leave one of his corps commanders in charge of the line at Savage Station. This lack of command unity enabled Heintzelman to march his *III Corps* to the south just as the Confederate attack was beginning against Sumner's front; for some reason Heintzelman thought that his mission for the day was completed and his troops were no longer needed on Sumner's left. Another "defection" occurred when Brigadier General Henry Slocum went over the head of his corps commander, William B. Franklin, to obtain permission from McClellan to withdraw to the south on the grounds that his men were still exhausted from their fight at Gaines' Mill two days earlier. In spite of the departure of so many troops, Sumner was chafing to mount a massive counterattack. He told Franklin, "I never leave a victorious field. Why! If I had twenty thousand more men, I would crush this rebellion." Sumner desperately sent a messenger to McClellan seeking authority to attack, only to receive the stern reply that he was to withdraw or be relieved of command. Sumner had no choice but to leave. His were the last troops to cross White Oak Swamp, and they destroyed the bridges behind them.

Sumner was actually fortunate to withdraw with his corps almost completely intact. Had Lee concentrated all his troops at Savage Station instead of swinging Longstreet's and A.P. Hill's divisions to the south along the Darbytown Road, he might have been able to give a sound defeat to McClellan's reinforced rear guard. The battle might also have gone in the Confederates favor had Magruder moved up more promptly and had Huger given him more support on the right. But the greatest Confederate disappointment was once again "Stonewall" Jackson. For various reasons Jackson had taken all day to repair the Grapevine Bridge, and his troops did not cross until the wee hours of 30 June. Nor was he enterprising enough to locate a useable ford situated nearby. Had he crossed the Chickahominy and come to Magruder's assistance, the Confederates would surely have won the battle of Savage Station. As the battle turned out, it was simply an inconclusive engagement, a rear guard action that featured lost opportunities by both sides. Final casualty figures for the day were about 700 Confederates and 500 Federals. In addition, some 1,100 Union soldiers were reported to be captured or missing during the army's retreat that day, and another 2,500 badly wounded men from the battles of Seven Pines and Gaines' Mill had to be left behind in hospitals.

McClellan's Generals

A contributing factor to McClellan's failure in the Peninsular Campaign was the lack of initiative and aggressiveness shown by his corps commanders. These five generals were the senior officers the army possessed, but all were equally inexperienced at handling large bodies of troops, and two (Heintzelman and Sumner) were too old for active field service. It is revealing to observe that none of the five still held their post six months later. All were retired or assigned administrative duties as younger, more talented commanders came to the fore. Some were removed also because of their close alliance with McClellan, after they fell into disfavor because of his failures and those of his close friend Ambrose E. Burnside.

The most able of McClellan's corps commanders may have been Brigadier General Fitz-John Porter (1822-1901, West Point 1845) of the *V Corps*. Porter began the war as a high ranking staff officer, and then led a division of the *III Corps* from October 1861 until he was named commander of the *V Corps* when it was formed on 18 May 1862. He led his men well at Mechanicsville and Gaines' Mill in the face of superior enemy forces. He was present but not heavily engaged at Second Bull Run and Antietam. Porter was loyal to his friend McClellan and made no secret of his disdain for John Pope, the losing Federal commander at Second Bull Run. This caused Pope to charge him with disobeying orders at the battle, and in the ensuing trial Porter ended up being made the scapegoat for Pope's defeat. Porter was cashiered in January 1863, but he had his case reexamined in 1878 and was finally reinstated in 1886. He was a cousin of the noted naval commander in the war, Admiral David Dixon Porter.

Major General William B. Franklin (1823-1903; he ranked first in the West Point Class of 1843) also suffered from his close association with McClellan. He led a brigade at First Bull Run and then a division until McClellan made him commander of the *VI Corps* when it was formed on 18 May 1862. He handled his troops well enough during the Seven Days Battles, after which he missed Second Bull Run and was present but not see a great deal of action at Antietam. Burnside elevated him to command of the army's *Left Grand Division* which he led at Fredericksburg. His criticism of Burnside's handling of the battle caused him to be made a scapegoat for the defeat by the Congressional Committee on the Conduct of the War. As a result he was exiled to the war's western theater, where he led the *XIX Corps* during Banks' unsuccessful Red River campaign. He was wounded at the battle of Sabine Crossroads on 8 April 1864 and retired from field service at the close of the campaign.

Major General Edwin Sumner of the *II Corps* (1797-1863) was an average commander who at age 65 was too old for field command. During the Peninsular Campaign his performance was erratic—he showed initiative at Seven Pines but was disappointing at Williamsburg. He also did not keep good control of his divisions at Antietam. Burnside promoted him to command of the army's *Right Grand Division* during the Fredericksburg campaign. He was briefly considered for the command of the Union army when Burnside was fired in January 1863, but let it be known that he wanted to retire. He died of natural causes two months later.

McClellan's other two corps commanders, Major Generals Samuel P. Heintzelman (1805-1880, West Point Class of 1826) and Erasmus Keyes (1810-1895, West Point Class of 1832) were less than satisfactory during the campaign. Heintzelman, commander of the *III Corps*, was personally brave but lacked initiative. The good fighting done by his troops during the campaign was due almost totally to the skills of his division commanders, Brigadier Generals Phil Kearny and Joe Hooker, not to Heintzelman's direction. After Second Bull Run he was moved to an administrative job for a year as commander of the troops defending Washington. In 1864 he was transferred to the Northern Department to fight Indians. Keyes, commander of the *IV Corps*, did not perform well at Williamsburg and positioned his troops poorly at Seven Pines. His corps was eventually discontinued after the campaign, and Keyes for a time commanded the troops at Yorktown and Suffolk. He was shelved in July 1863 and retired in May 1864.

McClellan's division commanders proved to be much better leaders during the campaign than the five corps commanders. Five of the army's nine division leaders would rise to corps command later in the war (John Sedgwick, Darius Couch, George Sykes, Henry Slocum, and W.F. Smith) and one, Joe Hooker, would be promoted to command the *Army of the Potomac* in 1863. In addition, four brigade commanders (Dan Butterfield, John Reynolds, Winfield Hancock) would also rise to command corps, and one, George G. Meade, would become the longest tenured commander of the *Army of the Potomac* (1863-1865). Another brigadier, Oliver O. Howard, would not only achieve corps command, but would later head the *Army of the Tennessee* during Sherman's campaigns in 1864 and 1865. The army's best overall division commander in the campaign may have been one-armed Brigadier General Phil Kearny. Kearny was promoted to major general on 4 July 1862 before having his career ended by a fatal Confederate bullet at the battle of Chantilly on 1 September 1862.

CHAPTER XII

Frayser's Farm

Sumner's withdrawal from the battlefield of Savage Station
was a difficult march, conducted in the dark over narrow
roads newly muddied by the thunderstorm that had brought
the battle to an early conclusion. His men moved south at
2200 and stumbled along all night along the causeways
through White Oak Swamp. It was Sumner's good fortune
that the Confederates did not pursue his long and vulnerable
column. Magruder had gone to sleep for the first time in two
days after establishing contact with Jackson's troops at 0330
on 30 June, and his pickets did not discover Sumner's withdrawal until after dawn. Huger's command was the Confederate unit best situated to intercept Sumner's line of march.
During his advance down the Charles City Road, his troops
had located one of the Federals' retreat routes across White
Oak Swamp, but Huger was wary of being isolated or sur-
rounded if he pushed forward too far. For this reason he
allowed his troops to go into bivouac at Brightwell's, located
east of White's Tavern and only two miles from one of the two
major roads on which the Yankees were retreating.

Sumner's weary troops completed their crossing by 1000
on 30 June and safely joined the rest of McClellan's army on
the south side of White Oak Swamp. The Union force, however, was not yet out of jeopardy. The army's long trains had
cleared their most dangerous obstacle, but were still strung
out for eight miles between the swamp and the James River.
This meant that McClellan had to form up to fight one more

195

Thomas J. "Stonewall" Jackson. Though one of the most brilliant generals of the War Between the States, Jackson's performance on the Peninsula was less than exemplary.

rear guard action before he could withdraw his entire command to the defensive lines his engineers were preparing on Malvern Hill, four miles directly south of the swamp. McClellan spent all morning on 30 June stationing his troops. Two divisions, Richardson's of Sumner's corps and Smith's of Franklin's corps, were assigned to block the two principal routes across White Oak Swamp. They were formed facing north immediately south of the swamp. The rest of the army faced east in a line that formed a right angle to Smith's division and then ran south to Malvern Hill. It was held by the following divisions from north to south: Slocum's of Franklin's corps, Kearny's of Heintzelman's corps, McCall's of Porter's corps, then Hooker's of Heintzelman's corps, supported by Sedgwick's of Sumner's corps. Morell's and Sykes' weakened divisions of Porter's corps were placed on the western crest of Malvern Hill, while Keyes' two divisions were stationed in general reserve on the northern slopes of the hill.

After completing his dispositions, McClellan held a late morning conference with Sumner, Heintzelman and Franklin to explain his plans for the day. He expected the three generals to hold off any Confederate attacks that might develop so that all of the army's wagons would have time to reach their new supply base at Harrison's Landing, located on the James River six miles southeast of Malvern Hill. The troops could then withdraw that night to Malvern Hill, where they could effectively block any further Confederate pursuit. The conference ended about noon, just as the sound of skirmish fire began crackling to signal the approach of Lee's army. Strange to say, McClellan did not stay to supervise the pending battle, but instead rode south to oversee the preparation of Porter's lines on Malvern Hill. At about 1700 he boarded the gunboat *Galena* and headed upstream a short distance in order to shell the right flank of the Confederates who were approaching Malvern Hill. These were indeed odd movements for an army commander in the midst of a serious campaign. Perhaps he did not anticipate any major fighting to develop north of Malvern Hill; if any combat did occur, he seems to have trusted, in Napoleonic manner, that his "marshals" would be able to deal with the situation. He may also have felt, as he told his wife, that his life was too valuable to the army and the country to expose it to danger in battle. That may be the reason why he did not expose himself to enemy fire during the campaign.

Lee was determined to continue his pursuit of McClellan's retreating army on 30 June and correctly deduced that the Union troops would head directly toward the James. He ordered most of his divisions to continue on the roads they had followed the previous day and strike the Yankees wherever they were encountered. He hoped that the converging road network would enable his units to catch McClellan's army strung out on the roads south of White Oak Swamp, and would also enable them to outflank and overwhelm the Federal rear guard. Jackson was ordered to march directly south from the Grapevine Bridge and continue on past White Oak Swamp until he encountered the enemy. Huger's line of march would be down the Charles City Road, while Long-

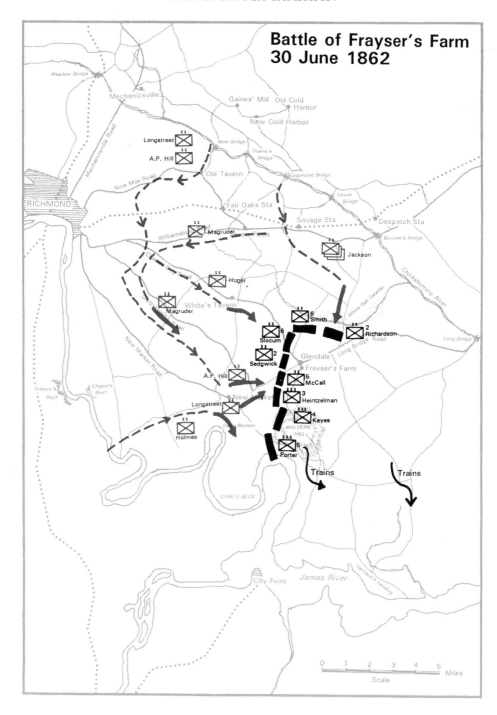

Battle of Frayser's Farm
30 June 1862

street and A. P.Hill
headed down the
New Market Road.
Holmes' newly ar-
rived division was to
head for Malvern
Hill via the road clos-
est to the James
River. The longest
march of the day
would be made by
Magruder's com-
mand, which was di-
rected to march west
from Savage Station
and take the Wil-

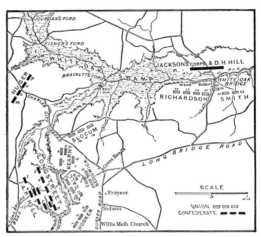

Tactical Map of Battle of Frayser's Farm

liamsburg Road almost to Richmond, where it would pick up
the Darbytown Road and head directly southeast toward the
James. This circuitous route was deemed necessary because a
march directly south from Savage Station would have
brought Magruder into two obstacles, the morass of White
Oak Swamp and the rear of Jackson's command. It is strange,
though, that Lee did not direct Magruder to march south from
Seven Pines on a lesser used road rather than making a five
mile long detour to pick up the Darbytown Road. The converging road net would lead Huger's, Longstreet's, A.P. Hill's
and Magruder's commands to a little crossroads called Glendale, located at the intersection of the Charles City and Long
Bridge Roads two miles north of Malvern Hill and an equal
distance south of White Oak Swamp. Lee understood that this
would be the most likely spot for the next battle.

Lee met personally with Jackson near Savage Station soon
after dawn to explain his strategy for the day. Though Jackson
had been up since a rain shower drenched his camp at 0100,
he seemed alert and ready for action. A Virginia artilleryman,
Robert Stiles, witnessed their brief conference: "Jackson flung

himself off his horse and advanced to meet Lee, the little sorrel trotting back to the staff...The two generals greeted each other warmly, but wasted no time upon the greeting...Jackson began talking in a jerky, impetuous way, meanwhile drawing a diagram on the ground with the toe of his right boot. He traced two sides of a triangle...Then began to draw a third slowly and with hesitation, alternately looking up at Lee's face and down at his diagram, meanwhile talking earnestly; and when at last...the triangle was complete he raised his foot and stamped it down with emphasis saying, 'We've got him;' then signaled for his horse and...vaulted awkwardly into the saddle and was off..."

In spite of Jackson's enthusiasm, he did not press his advance that morning as he had the many marches that his earned his division the nickname "Foot Cavalry" for their efforts in the Valley Campaign. To be certain, the roadways were narrow and well muddied by the passage of thousands of Union troops only a few hours before. In addition, many of the Confederates were distracted by all the abandoned Federal equipment they passed; other troops had to be assigned to guard over a thousand enemy stragglers that were taken in. These reasons combined to cause Jackson to consume all morning in traveling the eight or nine miles from Grapevine Bridge to the White Oak Swamp crossings.

Jackson's advance reached White Oak Swamp bridge, the eastern of the two primary crossings over the swamp, at 1200, just two hours after the last of Sumner's troops had crossed and rendered the bridge unusable. Jackson was not pleased to see Union guns and infantry formed up south of the bridge; they were obviously placed to cover the withdrawal of the wagons he saw in the distance moving slowly to the south. Jackson was not rash enough to begin an attack before he had sufficient infantry up. For the meanwhile, he decided to shell the enemy lines and began looking for a good position at which to post his guns. It was 1345 by the time he located a suitable open field three-quarters of a mile northwest of the

*W. F. Smith's division of the **VI** Corps engaged as a rear guard at White Oak Swamp. Lee's forces managed to rupture the Union line during the battle, but quick Federal action saved the day before the Confederates could exploit their success.*

bridge and began posting a line that would include 28 guns. Their concentrated fire wrecked most of a Union battery and drove off its supporting infantry. Elated, Jackson sent the 2nd Virginia Cavalry charging across the swamp to claim three damaged and abandoned guns. The horsemen crossed the swamp easily but were soon hit by heavy fire from positions that Jackson had not been able to see before. "Stonewall" himself had followed his cavalry across the swamp and was lucky to beat a safe but hasty retreat back with them.

Jackson ordered his artillery to open fire on the newly discovered Union position, but this time the Yankees did not flee. Instead, they replied with still more artillery and even forced Jackson to withdraw his infantry into a woods for

The murky wilderness of the Chickahominy Swamp.

shelter. By then Jackson was feeling too tired to deal with the swamp, the broken bridge, and the strongly posted enemy, so he lay down and went to sleep!

Nor did "Stonewall's" nap refresh him. When he awoke at about 1600 he seemed lethargic and unable to cope with the situation he faced. He did not press harder when the volunteers sent to repair the bridge were driven off by enemy fire. Likewise he did not search for other fords across the swamp, and he even discounted a report of another crossing located by a cavalry officer. Most amazing of all is the fact that he directed Brigadier General Wade Hampton to build a narrow pole bridge across the swamp, and then simply walked away

202

when Hampton reported that the project was finished! Jackson clearly was suffering from utter exhaustion, a weariness so complete that he fell asleep during supper with a cracker still in his mouth.

His dazed condition caused his 18,000 good troops to conduct no more than light skirmishing all afternoon and evening even though he was under orders to pursue and engage the enemy. This was the fourth time in five days that "Stonewall" failed to carry out Lee's orders.

Magruder also had his share of problems that day. He had not been feeling well personally for several days because of indigestion, and the morphine mixture his doctor gave him only irritated his system further. As a result, he could not sleep and was too sick and weary to think straight. Shortly after sunrise he received personal instructions from Lee to head back towards Richmond and then take the Darbytown Road to the southeast. He experienced some difficulty getting his troops into a line of march because they were tired and disorganized from their fight of the previous day. His start was further delayed until his guides came up. Once under way, he made good time until early afternoon, when he ran into the rear of A.P. Hill's column, which was halted on the Darbytown Road about six miles out from Richmond. After waiting in vain for two hours for Hill to move, Magruder received an order from Longstreet, the senior officer in that sector, to march south to support Holmes' command near the James River. He started his column moving again about 1630, only to receive an order from Lee to advance to the east and form on the right of Longstreet's command. Since most of his troops had already reached New Market on their way to support Holmes, they had to be countermarched towards Glendale. By the time they started to come up, it was dark and too late to go into action. Magruder's men were on the road for 18 hours this day, covering some 20 miles and none fired a shot.

Jackson and Magruder were not the only Confederate

"Stonewall" Jackson's Health during the Campaign

There is no question that "Stonewall" Jackson's performance during the Seven Days Battles was disappointing to General Lee, especially in view of the promise he had shown at Bull Run and the brilliance he exhibited during his spring 1862 Shenandoah Valley campaign. Jackson uncharacteristically arrived late at Mechanicsville, got lost on his way to Gaines' Mill, and did not show initiative at White Oak Swamp and Malvern Hill. Historians have offered various explanations for Jackson's subpar performance—that he was exhausted from the rigors of the Valley campaign, that he was totally unfamiliar with the terrain around Richmond, that he was not used to coordinating his movements with other large bodies of troops, and that he did not want to expose his battle weary men to un-

necessary combat.

The most enlightening examination of Jackson's poor performance during the campaign has been made by noted historian Douglas Southall Freeman in an appendix to volume II of his detailed biography entitled *R.E. Lee*. Freeman did a study of how much sleep Jackson got during the last nine days of June 1862 and argued convincingly that Jackson was exhausted from a lack of rest, particularly by sleepless nights on 22-23 June, 23-24 June, and 25-26 June, that clouded his thinking and sapped his physical strength and intellectual vigor. Major R.L. Dabney of Jackson's staff also noted that Jackson did not eat well during this period. His headquarters wagon, mess chest and cook were all left behind at Hundley's Corner on 27 June, and neither Jackson nor his staff

commanders having another bad day. Huger had his troops up at dawn and sent them slowly down the Charles City Road because of a false report that there was a large Union unit in the White Oak Swamp or to the north of the swamp. After he thoroughly scouted the ground to his left to make sure that it was safe to go forward, his advance came under Union skirmish fire. Then he ran into a more serious obstacle, a number of trees felled across the road. Brigadier General William Mahone, commander of Huger's leading brigade, thought that it would be easier to cut a new road through the woods

members drew rations or had regular meals for the next five days.
A summary of Freeman's outline

Jackson's activities for the end of
June 1862 is as follows:

Night of 22-23 June: No sleep; left at 0100 to ride to Richmond
Day of 23 June: Rode to Lee's headquarters, had conference, started re-
turn trip to his troops.
Night of 23-24 June: Rode all night; he covered a total of 100 miles in the
previous 24 hours.
Day of 24 June: A long and difficult march towards Richmond.
Night of 24-25 June: Slept but got up early to continue march.
Day of 25 June: March to Ashland.
Night of 25-26 June: Did not sleep; stayed up all night to pray and give or-
ders.
Day of 26 June: Marched from Ashland to Hundley's Corner; retired
early instead of entering battle at Mechanicsville.
Night of 26-27 June: Up at crack of dawn.
Day of 27 June: Got lost marching to battlefield near Gaines' Mill; fought
battle.
Night of 27-28 June: Got some sleep before midnight, when he conferred
with Stuart.
Day of 28 June: Spent at Gaines' Mill battlefield.
Night of 28-29 June: Probably his best night's sleep that week.
Day of 29 June: Rebuilt Grapevine Bridge.
Night of 29-30 June: Slept until awakened by rainstorm at 0100; did not
go back to sleep.
Day of 30 June: Marched to White Oak Swamp Bridge; fell asleep with a
cracker in his mouth while eating dinner.
Night of 30 June - 1 July: Perhaps got a full night's sleep.
Day of 1 July: Marched to Malvern Hill and fought battle there.

for the artillery to use than it would be to chop through the
barrier on the road, so he set his axmen to work.

A shortage of axes made the job painfully slow, and gave
the Yankees time to fell even more trees on the road farther
ahead of Mahone. Huger would have been better advised to
leave his artillery behind and advance only his infantry. As it
was, the slow progress of his tree choppers brought his column to a crawl while the Union trains lumbered south to
safety just two miles away. When he finally reached the Union
rear guard about 1400, he brought up his precious artillery

and began shelling the enemy, even though he outnumbered the Union forces that faced him. His command, like Jackson's, was brought to a halt for the day.

The only Confederate column to reach its destination on time on 30 June was Longstreet's. He marched to the end of the Darbytown Road as ordered and then turned east on the Long Bridge Road. About 1100 he encountered McCall's and Kearny's Union divisions drawn up west of Glendale (also known as Charles City Crossroads). Longstreet formed his men into battle line, keeping A.P. Hill's division in reserve as it came up to the end of the Darbytown Road. His men began skirmishing, but Longstreet felt that the ground was too densely wooded and unfavorable to make an attack. He decided to await the arrival of Huger's force, which was expected at any moment to approach Glendale from the northwest along the Charles City Road.

As already noted, Huger did not approach the Union lines northwest of Glendale until 1400. When his guns began firing at 1430, Longstreet thought that they were a signal that Huger was ready to attack, and directed his batteries to fire in acknowledgement. Longstreet's salvo brought a reply from the Union guns facing him and precipitated a brief artillery engagement. At that moment Longstreet and A.P. Hill were conferring with General Lee and President Davis, who had once again come out from Richmond to see the fighting. The group was too near the front and was peppered with Union shells, one of which killed a courier and several horses. Longstreet noted in his memoirs that "the little clearing was speedily cleared of the distinguished group that graced its meagre soil." When Longstreet sent some sharpshooters forward to silence the Union battery, skirmishing became even heavier across his entire front. Lee, however, kept the conflict from escalating further because he was waiting for Huger and Jackson to begin their scheduled attacks. Once they entered action, he would release A.P. Hill's rested division and overwhelm the enemy lines.

While Lee was waiting for Huger and Jackson to attack, he received a report from cavalry Colonel Thomas L. Rosser that a Union column was moving south across Malvern Hill. Lee became fearful that the enemy might be slipping away, so he rode south to see for himself what the situation was. After learning that there was a Union force posted on Malvern Hill, he ran into some of Holmes' artillery moving forward from the New Market Heights. Holmes had crossed the James on 29 June and by 1000 on 30 June had his makeshift division of about 6,000 men from the defenses south of Richmond posted at New Market to guard the junction of the Long Bridge and River Roads. Holmes had not felt that his force was strong enough to engage the enemy by himself, so he had held his position in order to await developments. Around 1600 he heard the same reports that had reached Lee, that the enemy was retreating across Malvern Hill, and decided to send forward his artillery to harass the Union retreat. These were the guns that Lee came upon at about 1630. Lee at once went to see Holmes and urge him to open fire with his cannons as soon as he brought up all his infantry.

Unfortunately for the Confederates, Holmes' advancing column raised so much dust that the Union forces on Malvern Hill (most of Porter's corps) were easily alerted to their approach. The Yankees manned their cannons and opened fire with long range shells. The barrage caught Holmes' men totally unprepared, and the Confederates initially could not even tell where the shells were coming from. Noisy blasts from the Union gunboats in the James added to the confused scene. The Confederates, all of whom were entering their first battle, were totally rattled. At least one regiment, the 45th North Carolina, broke and ran; everyone else dove for cover. The cannoneers of one reserve battery panicked and fled, leaving two cannons and three caissons abandoned on the road.

At length General Holmes rode up into the din. He was partially deaf and thought that he had heard some firing!

Holmes restored order and posted his artillery to fire on the Union wagons that were still crossing Malvern Hill; the wagons were actually the tail end of McClellan's long column heading for Harrison's Landing. As soon as his guns opened fire—it was now after 1800—they were blasted by Federal salvoes that were heavier than what had previously greeted his infantry. Holmes had no way of knowing that Union Colonel Henry J. Hunt, head of McClellan's reserve artillery, had posted a number of his heavy guns, including eight 20-pounder Parrots and a few siege pieces, on Malvern Hill in order to protect the army's withdrawal. Holmes' guns were no match in number or calibre to the Union fire power, and suffered heavily before they were withdrawn about an hour later. By that time Holmes had rightly decided that it would be "perfect madness" to order his infantry to assault the Union position. He kept his men in line until after sunset so that they could withdraw under the protecting cover of darkness, and pulled back at 2100 to New Market Heights.

After sending Holmes' division forward at 1630, Lee returned to Longstreet's front and found that there was still no news from Huger and Jackson. Despairing that the Yankees would escape unscathed if nothing were done, Lee ordered Longstreet to attack; he hoped that the sound of his assault would hurry Huger and Jackson to attack also. Longstreet's men were ready to go. The center of their attack struck McCall's Pennsylvania division, which was posted behind a stream on the south side of Long Bridge Road, about half a mile west of Glendale and Frayser's Farm. McCall's men had seen heavy fighting at Mechanicsville and Gaines' Mill, and were tired out from their halting marches during the withdrawal to the James. Nevertheless they withstood Longstreet's initial charge well because the Confederate advance was, as the general admitted later, "very much broken up by the rough ground we had to move over, and we were not in sufficiently solid form to maintain a proper battle line."

At several points McCall's men managed to mount counterattacks that blunted and drove back Longstreet's attackers. The fighting was particularly fierce around Kern's and Cooper's batteries of the *1st Pennsylvania Artillery*. Private John Luban of the *1st Pennsylvania Reserves* described the action: "With a loud cheer we rushed on the advancing enemy. We did not fire a shot, but relying on the bayonet we charged with an impetuosity that broke the rebel line, when we poured a deadly volley into their backs and pursued them over the field. Unfortunately, the momentum of the charge carried us too far, and it soon became evident that we had got ourselves in a bad fix. A column of fresh rebel troops flanked us...and we were compelled to fall back in confusion to the edge of a wood in the rear of Cooper's battery. The enemy in strong force now rushed on the battery, and, capturing it, were on the point of turning the guns on our lines when Colonel Roberts ordered us to take cover behind the trees and open on the enemy." The *1st Reserves* fought until it was almost overwhelmed, when it received timely reinforcements in the form of the *9th Pennsylvania Reserves*. The Federals "with a tremendous cheer charged upon the enemy, and a most terrible conflict ensued. Both sides discharged their pieces, and then with the most frantic yells of rage rushed on each other. Never was battle more severely contested...No time could be secured for loading, so all had to rely on the bayonet or such weapons as they might have in their possession. Bayonet thrusts were frequently given, muskets clubbed, and even knives were used in this fearful struggle. The dead bodies of men and horses and broken caissons were literally piled up around the guns of the battery, and in some cases afforded barricades for the contestants."

Soon battle raged all along the line. Jenkins' South Carolina brigade made three mad rushes into canister blasts from Randol's battery of the *1st U.S. Artillery* before they finally captured it. Both sides committed reinforcements, Sedgwick's division from the Union side, A.P. Hill's from the Confederate side. One Union volley felled 75 men of the 40th Virginia.

The charge of Confederates of the 55th and 60th Virginia wins a battery of Yankee cannons during the fight at Frayser's Farm.

When the 60th Virginia reached the Union lines, four Federals bayonetted Private Robert Christian; before he died he killed three of his assailants and his brother dispatched the fourth. One Pennsylvania soldier wrote of the terrific contest: "Bayonets thrust and parried; muskets were clubbed; pistols, daggers and bowie knives were freely used as the hostile currents surged in the turmoil of death, around and among the guns and caissons."

When Kearny's Union division mounted a counterattack, it seemed that McClellan's men would carry the day. A.P. Hill saw them coming and hurried to the front lines to rally Branch's brigade, which was starting to break. He boldly seized the flag of the 7th North Carolina and shouted, "Damn you, if you will not follow me, I'll die alone!" His bravado succeeded and the line held. He then committed his last reserve, J.R. Anderson's Georgia brigade. Hill ordered his men to cheer as loudly as they could in order to deceive the Yan-

*Slocum's artillery engages in a duel with their Confederate coun-
terparts during Frayser's Farm. Behind them is the* **16th New
York** *attempting to weather the engagement by lying down.*

kees as to their strength. The ruse worked. Anderson's men
charged towards the Union line and held their fire until they
were within 70 paces of the enemy, whereupon they opened
fire and yelled like a tribe of Indians. The Yankee line on this
front disintegrated within five minutes, but was soon shored
up by other troops.

The fighting continued until well after dark, with neither
side gaining a distinct advantage. In spite of the din, neither
Huger nor Jackson moved to enter the fight. Their inactivity
enabled Richardson's Union division to withdraw from Jackson's front and come to McCall's aid. When the firing finally

began to sputter out, the Union lines still held and Lee had lost another chance to crush McClellan's retreating army. Longstreet's and A.P. Hill's divisions had fought well, but they suffered heavily as the attackers and lost over 3,300 men. Union losses amounted to 2,853, of which 1,130 were captured. Among the latter was Brigadier General George McCall, who had mistakenly ridden up to the 47th Virginia in the twilight. A Confederate volley had felled most of his staff, and he had to rush to surrender in order to avoid being shot.

The last Confederate attack was made at twilight by Kershaw's and Semmes' brigades. The heavy smoke and growing darkness made it so difficult to see that the attackers were struck from friendly fire from the rear, whereupon they had to withdraw. The infantry firing on both sides continued on until about 2100, when the rest of the weary Confederate units began to withdraw. Union artillery fire went on for about another hour until the battle finally came to a conclusion.

CHAPTER XIII

Malvern Hill

*M*cClellan's absence from the battlefield of Frayser's Farm caused some difficulties when the fighting there began to die out about an hour after dark on 30 June 1862. The corps commanders on the field realized that they were in an awkward situation and that Lee would surely continue the battle in the morning, yet no one had orders to quit the field. About 2100 Major General William Franklin, commander of the *VI Corps*, took it on his own responsibility to withdraw his command south towards Malvern Hill, where most of Porter's *V Corps* and Hunt's reserve artillery had just driven off Holmes' feeble attack. Franklin informed Major General Samuel Heintzelman, commander of the *III Corps*, of his decision, and Heintzelman, too, prepared to leave. Their departure left Major General Edwin Sumner, commander of the *II Corps*, with no choice but to follow. The Union withdrawal was not contested by the Confederates.

The Federal troops completed their withdrawal to Malvern Hill by daylight on 1 July and were posted in a very strong defensive posture on Malvern Hill. The hill was a broad plateau about three-quarters of a mile broad and over a mile deep with plenty of room for posting troops. Its slopes were well guarded and offered only one clear route of access. The southern slope of the hill abutted the James River, the eastern slope was fronted by Western Run and thick underbrush, and the hill's western slope was protected by forests and a swamp along Turkey Run. The position was accessible

McClellan oversees the placement of batteries on Malvern Hill. Malvern Hill would prove to be the only substantial Federal victory of the Peninsula campaign.

only on its northern face, and here the ground rose fairly sharply to the hill's sixty foot height.

McClellan had more than enough men to defend the hilltop in depth. He spent the night of 30 June-1 July at Porter's headquarters on the southern edge of the hill, and was up at dawn to complete his dispositions. Hunt's artillery, which had fought so well against Holmes the night before, was kept in position above Turkey Run. Franklin's corps was posted on the eastern face of the hill above Western Run. Almost all the rest of the infantry was formed in several lines on the open northern face of the hill, the only practical attack route for the Confederates. Morell's division of Porter's corps occupied the left end of the line, between the Crew House and the

Greenclad members of Colonel Hiram Berdan's U.S. Sharpshooters skirmish with Confederates of Armistead's brigades during the battle of Malvern Hill.

Quaker Road; its three brigades were formed successively behind a long row of cannons, and the entire division was supported by the two brigades of U.S. Regulars from Sykes' division. Couch's division of Keyes' *IV Corps* was deployed at the center of the line, a little bit in advance of Morell's lines so as to permit the artillery behind to fire over it. Heintzelman's corps supported Couch's center and right, and extended the main line east to Western Run. Sumner's corps formed yet a third line near the Binford House and connected with Franklin's corps along Western Run. The Pennsylvania Reserves were held in general reserve on the southern edge of the hill, and one brigade of Sykes' division guarded the River Road bridge over Turkey Run. The position was the strongest the army had held during the entire campaign, with over 80,000 troops supported by 250 cannons and the gunboats on the James. The weary Union foot soldiers, tired and demoralized by three days of retreating and rear guard actions, recognized the strength of the position, and their spirits at last began to improve. Hundreds of exhausted stragglers were seen streaming up the hillside on their way to rejoin their regiments.

McClellan had no intention of remaining long on Malvern Hill, despite the strength of the position. He intended it to be only a delaying post on the last stage of the army's withdrawal to his new base at Harrison's Landing, six miles to the southeast. On the morning of 1 July he wrote to General Dix at Fort Monroe to ask for reinforcements and observed that his men "were in no condition to fight without 24 hours rest...I pray that the enemy may not be in condition to disturb us today." McClellan was clearly a beaten man, and had no intention of striking back at Lee; his only goal was to save his command from what he believed to be a vastly superior enemy force. After giving instructions to Brigadier General A.A. Humphreys, his chief topographical engineer, to oversee the completion of the lines on Malvern Hill, McClellan boarded the gunboat *Galena* at 0915 and headed for Harrison's Landing. His intention was to oversee the preparation of the new lines there, but once again he was deliberately absenting himself from the army when a battle was pending.

Shortly after dawn on 1 July Lee held a conference at Willis Church with his five principal lieutenants, Longstreet, Jackson (who had at last gotten a little sleep), Magruder (who was still sick), A.P. Hill and D.H. Hill. Holmes was too far distant to attend, and Huger was absent because he had not yet discovered that the Yankees had withdrawn from his front. Lee himself was tired and a bit unwell; he was also disappointed that his plans had gone awry so many times. Nevertheless, he was determined to continue to press McClellan while he had the Yankees on the run. He had a strong suspicion that McClellan would hold on to Malvern Hill that day to allow his wagons more time to head downriver, so he ordered his officers to advance and prepare for battle. Lee had hopes of catching and destroying whatever rear guard McClellan left behind, and he did not expect the demoralized Yankees to put up much of a fight. D.H. Hill was the only officer present to object to an attack on Malvern Hill. He had learned of the position's strength from a chaplain who lived in the area, and wisely advised Lee, "If General McClellan is there in force, we had better let him alone." Longstreet did not take the argument seriously and replied to Hill, "Don't get scared, now we have him licked."

Lee decided that Jackson and Magruder should lead the army's advance to Malvern Hill. Huger would be sent forward when he came up, and Longstreet and A.P. Hill, who had been heavily engaged the day before at Frayser s Farm, would be held in reserve. Magruder offered to take the lead, but Jackson argued that his troops were fresher and won the honor.

After Lee's conference adjourned, Jackson began leading his men south past the Frayser's Farm battlefield and took the Willis Church Road (also called the Quaker Road) south towards Malvern Hill. On the way he encountered a large number of Union skirmishers who delayed his arrival until late morning. As soon as the Confederates came within sight of the Union troops, the Federal cannons opened fire. The firing continued as Jackson formed his troops. He assigned Whiting's two brigades to the front line left of the Quaker Road, and D.H. Hill's division was placed west of the road; Jackson's old division and most of Ewell's were held in reserve. Skirmishing intensified while Jackson formed his lines, as did the Union artillery fire. One shot decapitated a man seated near General D.H. Hill. One of his brigadiers, John B. Gordon, saw what happened and urged Hill to seek cover. Hill replied, "Don't worry about me, look after the men. I am not going to get killed until my time comes." No sooner had he spoken than another shell exploded near him and knocked him over in the dirt. Hill calmly dusted himself off and went behind a tree for cover.

Jackson completed his dispositions by 1100 and began looking for Magruder, who was supposed to be forming on his right. Magruder, however, was nowhere to be seen. It seems that he had told his guides to lead him by the Quaker Road, as Lee had ordered, but the guides had led him to a different Quaker Road off the Long Bridge Road. Magruder's march led him past Longstreet's camp, and that general argued strongly to "Prince John" that he was headed in the wrong direction. Magruder nevertheless insisted that his guides were right. Their impasse continued until a messenger came from Lee with orders for Magruder to return the way he had come and form on Jackson's right. His countermarch delayed the start of the battle greatly and forced Lee to deploy Huger's command on Jackson's right instead. When Magruder finally did reach the front, his men were placed in a second line behind Huger and the right of D.H. Hill's position.

The Confederate officers were dismayed by the strength of the Union position, yet dutifully carried out Lee's instructions to prepare for an attack. At about 1330, Lee issued his battle orders, which he had formulated in conjunction with Longstreet. He ordered Magruder to form all the artillery he could on a hill east of the Quaker Road, and Jackson was directed to form his batteries in an open field on the Poindexter farm, about 1400 yards northeast of the center of the Union line. The two artillery positions would catch the Federal forces in a cross fire between them. When the moment was right, the infantry would rush to the assault, beginning from the right. His exact order read, "Batteries have been established to rake the enemy's line. If it is broken, as is probable, Armistead, who can witness the effect of the fire, has been ordered to charge with a yell. Do the same."

Lee's plan was not very ingenious, but it was the best he felt that he could do under the circumstances. He had wanted to explore the possibility of outflanking Malvern Hill to the east but needed Stuart's absent cavalry to scout the area; Stuart had been north of the Chickahominy for several days and still had not returned under an order issued late on 30 June. The principal weakness of Lee's attack order as issued lay in the fact that his army could not mass enough cannons to deal with the massed Union artillery on the hill. Jackson had an easier route to form his artillery on the Poindexter farm, but he experienced difficulty bringing up his batteries because his artillery chief, Stapleton Crutchfield, was ill and unable to be on duty. Jackson also had difficulty locating enough guns to bring up. It turned out that D.H. Hill had sent all of his guns back to Seven Pines to refit. Jackson should have been able to get some of the 20 batteries that General W.N. Pendleton had under his command in the army's artillery reserve, but he was unable to locate either Pendleton or the guns—they were caught up in a traffic jam on the Quaker Road more than a mile to the rear. As a result, Jackson was able to post only 18 guns, far less than the 100 that Longstreet thought would be necessary for the job. The situation was worse on the right, where the difficult ground prevented some units from advancing to their assigned position. The first battery commander to come up was reluctant to enter the action, and the second battery had only two guns with sufficient range to reach the enemy. Captain William Pegram with his six guns seemed to be the only artillerist capable of bringing up all his pieces for action on that flank.

The Union artillery had opened up at 1300 on the Confederate infantry even before the Southern artillery began to deploy. As Lee's batteries came up after 1330 and took position one by one, each fell under heavy enemy fire. The Con-

Battle of Malvern Hill
1 July 1862

TACTICAL MAP OF THE BATTLE OF MALVERN HILL

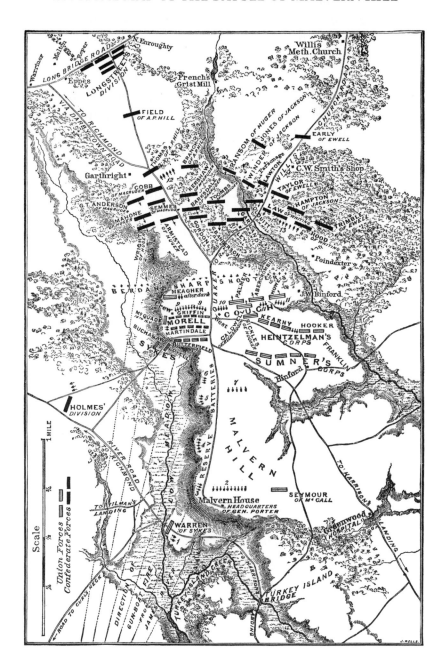

federate gunners continued the unequal contest as best they could for over an hour as piece after piece was knocked out of action. By 1500 Pegram had only one gun left, and he was helping to man it himself. Jackson's guns were also having a difficult time and gradually ceased firing by 1530. D.H. Hill thought that the promised artillery support was "farcical" and complained to Jackson, only to be ordered to be ready to attack when Armistead moved forward on the right. Lee was also very concerned about his artillery's ineffectiveness, and rode to see for himself if the Union position could be turned on the eastern side of the hill.

Lee might possibly have called the battle off if affairs had developed differently on his own right flank. As already noted, Lee's 1330 attack order had directed Armistead to keep an eye on the enemy and attack if he saw an opening, and the rest of the army would follow. During the afternoon's artillery duel, Armistead's men came under increasing heavy fire from the Union skirmishers (many from Hiram Berdan's elite greenclad regiment of U.S. Sharpshooters) on their front. Sometime after 1500 Armisted sent three of his regiments (38th, 14th and 53rd Virginia) to drive the annoying skirmishers back. The units carried out their objective "in handsome style," as Armistead reported, but "in their ardor they went too far." They were luckily able to obtain temporary shelter in a swale at the base of the hill. Armistead was in the process of figuring out what to do next when Magruder came up with his division, exhausted from all his countermarching, yet eager for battle. It was at this time that Magruder first received Lee's 1330 order to attack when Armistead raised a yell. Armistead was clearly engaged, as far as Magruder could see, so he hastily formed his men into battle line and sent a message to Lee that he was up and about to enter the fight.

Lee was returning from his reconnaissance on the left when he received Magruder's note. He had heard nothing directly from Armistead, so he took Magruder's report of

Armistead's advance at face value. If the Union line were weakened enough for Armistead to attack, it was time to launch a general assault, in spite of the continuing Union artillery fire. Lee's conclusion was strengthened by a report from Whiting, who claimed that he saw Union infantry pulling back from the enemy center (Sumner was actually shuffling his lines to protect them better from Confederate artillery fire). These messages from Magruder and Whiting led Lee to send an attack order to Magruder: "Press forward with your whole line and follow up Armistead's success."

Magruder for once reacted promptly to Lee's command, even though he did not have all his infantry or any of his artillery in position. At 1645 he directed Mahone's and Wright's brigades of Huger's division, about 2,500 men, to prepare to move forward towards the Union left at the Crew House. When the two brigades began advancing a short while later, they passed by Armistead's three regiments that were still in the ravine at the base of the hill. Armistead's men promptly joined the attack and gave out a rebel yell. The gray lines charged through a field full of shocked wheat amidst a growing fury of Union artillery and musketry fire. Only a few units, including the 12th Virginia, were able to advance as close as 150 yards to the Union position. The withering enemy fire was too much to bear and the Confederates were unable to mount a charge to reach the solid Federal lines that "stood as if on dress parade." Most of the attackers found that it was just as dangerous to withdraw as it was to advance, so they sought what cover they could and prayed for darkness to come.

The cheering of Armistead's attacking regiments caught D.H. Hill by surprise. He was already convinced that the Union position was too strong to be attacked successfully, and was not expecting to see any action. When he heard the rebel yell on his right, he exclaimed to his brigadiers, "Bring up your brigades as soon as possible and join in it."

Hill's experienced brigades began their attack at 1830. The

brave soldiers did not have a chance in the face of all the massed Union firepower that only been slightly weakened by the ineffective Confederate artillery. The attackers had to cross over half a mile of open fields straight into the face of the Union guns. The assault was to be every bit as bloody as Pickett's more famous charge at Gettysburg one year and two days later, and would fail for many of the same reasons.

G.B. Anderson's brigade, which was at the center of Hill's line, led the attack. One Union soldier described the bloody scene as follows: "The woods bordering our main field swarmed with gray and butternut coats, and regiments stepped briskly forward, firing as they moved. Our batteries spoke quick and often...Here and there a wide rent opens in the ordered files. It never closes, for another gap disorders the men who would try to fill the first. Our infantry add their galling fire to the crash of shells...No troops can stand such a fire, and the rebel brigade fell back under cover of the woods after half an hour of courageous effort."

Garland's and Ripley's brigades charged through blasts of canister so devastating that their men had no choice but to hit the ground for cover. The greatest success was achieved by Rodes' brigade, which was led during the battle by Colonel John B. Gordon. Despite taking heavy casualties—Union shells killed six and seven men at a time, and the 3rd Alabama lost half of its men—Gordon pushed back the first Union infantry line and advanced to within 200 yards of the enemy artillery. The fire they encountered was so heavy that they, too, had to seek shelter behind a swell; Gordon himself had his pistol handle broken, his canteen pierced, and his jacket ripped open by musket balls, but he was unhurt. He knew that his brigade was isolated and desperately called for reinforcements before he was counterattacked. Hill frantically sent Colquitt's 6th Georgia and all of Toombs' brigade forward. These troops were able to make it only as far as the brow of the hill before they broke and retreated under the enemy's withering fire.

A Federal gun in action at Malvern Hill. Federal artillery played a major part in this battle, melting away oncoming Confederate infantry with grapeshot and canister. Confederate D.H. Hill recalled, "It wasn't war, it was murder."

Jackson sent up his old division under Winder to support Hill's left at about 1900. By then Hill's attack was already in serious trouble. Winder noted that he ran into the most terrific fire he had ever seen, a continuous stream of shot, shell and balls that went on for two hours. His brigades and regiments were shattered, and here, too, the Confederates were forced to seek what shelter they could find as they waited for darkness to come and cover their retreat. Isaac Trimble of Ewell's division was the only brigadier on this front who was determined to carry through the assault as ordered. As he was forming to attack, Jackson rode up and held him back with the sad observation that D.H. Hill's entire division had just been repulsed and there was no sense in trying further.

While Jackson's and Hill's men were being decimated, Magruder succeeded at getting almost half of his and Huger's brigades into action. Unfortunately, he sent his units forward piecemeal as they came up and so conducted a series of disjointed, unsupported charges. D.H. Hill described the grisly scene: "They did not move together and were beaten in detail. As each brigade emerged from the woods, from 50 to 100 guns opened upon it, tearing great gaps in its ranks, but the heroes reeled on and were shot by the reserves at the guns...It was not war, it was murder."

The Union troops were elated at their opportunity to at last inflict a clear-cut defeat on the enemy. One soldier wrote that "cheer after cheer went up; shouts of triumph mingled with the peals of cannon and the clash of arms." The victory did not come, however, without great effort. One Union battery fired over 1,390 rounds during the day; the soldiers of the *105th Pennsylvania* had been issued 150 rounds of ammunition (they usually carried only 40 or 60) and they fired every bullet. In the *61st New York*, the men's gun barrels became so heated that they could not be touched and had to be held by their sling straps.

At various points along the lines, the Federals attempted limited counterattacks, though they could not advance far against the heavy Confederate infantry fire they encountered. Towards sunset, Porter received two brigades (Meagher's from Sumner's corps and Sickles' from Heintzelman's) to buttress his lines and used their regiments to relieve his units that had run out of ammunition. The *69th New York* of Meagher's Irish Brigade routed one Confederate regiment with a galling flank fire and received much praise for its charge after the battle. Porter went forward to view the action close up and lost his horse to enemy fire; he feared for awhile that he would be captured, so he destroyed his personal papers before he at last found a chance to return safely to his lines.

Lee still had about half of his army available, since he had not yet committed Whiting, Longstreet, A.P. Hill or Holmes to action. Wisely he let the battle come to a conclusion, recognizing that his men could not win this fight by valor alone. As darkness fell about 2100, the survivors of the bloody attacks began to withdraw as best they could. First the musketry fire died away, then the Union artillery ceased firing an hour later. All was quiet save for occasional skirmish fire and the pitiful cries of the wounded and dying.

The battle of Malvern Hill was indeed a bloody disaster for the Confederates, costing them 5,355 men. These casualties were entirely in vain, as McClellan most certainly would have abandoned Malvern Hill the next day without a fight in order to reconcentrate his army along the lines he had laid out at Harrison's Landing. Union losses in the battle amounted to 3,214: 397 killed, 2,092 wounded, and 725 missing. Most of the latter were wounded that had to be left behind when the army retreated during the night.

CHAPTER XIV

Harrison's Landing

*U*nion commander George B. McClellan had no intention of keeping his army at Malvern Hill, despite the ease of its victory on 1 July 1862. After arranging his troops that morning, McClellan had gone to Harrison's Landing at 0915 to oversee the sighting of his new position there. He returned to Malvern Hill late in the afternoon when he heard that a battle was imminent. Though he correctly surmised that the Confederate attack would hit his left, he took up a position almost two miles away on the army's right, claiming that he was apprehensive of an attack there. He made no effort to visit the scene of the fighting on the left, and at sunset returned to his temporary headquarters at Haxall's Landing. There, before conferring with Porter or any of the victorious generals at the front, he issued orders at 2100 for the army to withdraw to Harrison's Landing. That destination had been his goal for several days, and he had gathered all his supplies there and laid out good defensive lines. He fully expected to renew the campaign after he rested and refitted his troops and received reinforcements.

McClellan's withdrawal order reached Malvern Hill just as the fighting was drawing to a close. His generals were once again amazed to be ordered away from a victorious battlefield; fiery Phil Kearny told his staff that McClellan must have been guilty of either cowardice or treason. Porter thought that the position could be maintained and could be used as a base for the next several days. When he received the withdrawal

Supplies being distributed to a tired and exhausted **Army of the Potomac** *at Harrison's Landing.*

order he had just sent a message to McClellan reporting his victory and "expressing the hope that our withdrawal had ended and that we should hold the ground we now occupied, even if we did not assume the offensive." He dutifully began carrying out the order, and was careful to report his impending departure to Generals Heintzelman and Sumner so that they could cover him before they pulled back. McClellan had given him permission to spike his heavy guns if they could not be withdrawn, but this was not necessary. McClellan also advised him to try to cheer his men by informing them that reinforcements and fresh supplies were awaiting them at the end of their march.

The battle weary Union troops were filing off the hill before midnight. Torches set by the roadside were used to light the way as the exhausted men stumbled towards Harrison's Landing. Their depression was increased greatly the next morning when a storm blew in from the northeast that began drenching everyone with cold rain. The artillery and wagons soon turned the roadways into slippery mud, and the infantry had to slush through the adjoining fields as best they could. One soldier from the *19th Massachusetts* said that this march was one of the worst his regiment ever experienced. Another foot soldier claimed that he saw a mule disappear up to his ears in a mudhole, though he admitted that "it might have been a small mule."

The comfort of McClellan's men did not improve any when they reached Harrison's Landing. The army was bivouacked in a large wheat field near the Harrison mansion. The wheat was quickly trampled and the soil became a sticky paste in the cold and steady rain. The troops had no boards or wood to floor their tents and had to sleep in the mud. When the rain continued all night, the field was inundated by a myriad of small pools. To make matters worse, the loose soil would not hold the tent pins, and by the morning of 3 July, as George Kilmer of the *27th New York* reported, "The tents were nearly all down, exposing men whose beds were sinking deeper and deeper into the mud to the pelting rain."

The Confederates were not at all surprised to see the Federals retreat from Malvern Hill, and "Stonewall" Jackson had fully expected them to do so. At dawn on 2 July most of the Confederate troops were in their camps taking roll calls and licking their wounds; the only fresh Southern troops on the battlefield proper were men of Early's brigade, who occupied a bloody wheat field below the Yankee lines. Early's men saw a number of Federal troops still on the hill, but it was clear that most of the Union army was gone and this was only a rear guard. The Union force was commanded by Colonel W.W. Averell and consisted of the *3rd Pennsylvania Cavalry*, *67th New York Infantry*, and Buchanan's brigade of U.S. Regulars. Averell made a big show of actively moving his men

McClellan's Horses

General George B. McClellan's favorite mount was a dark bay named "Daniel Webster". The horse stood 17 hands high and was noted for his rapid gait. McClellan liked him because he had the stamina to trot all day. The general claimed that "Dan" was "never ill for an hour, never fatigued, never disturbed by fire," and only once lost his equanimity while in service. This was at Harrison's Landing at the close of the Peninsular campaign. McClellan was riding him through some abandoned works, when "Dan" "for the first time in his life gave vent to his feelings by a series of most vicious plunges and kicks. It was possible that the flies, who had enjoyed a whole army to feed on, concentrated all their energies on Dan; but I have always more than suspected that, in his quiet way, Dan understood the condition of affairs much better than the authorities at Washington, and merely wished to inform me in his own impressive manner that he fully agreed with my views as to the folly of abandoning the position, and that he, at least, had full confidence in his master."

"Dan" survived the war and lived on until 1879. McClellan was pleased that the old horse continued to recognize his master until the day he died.

Because of the rigors of army service, it was always necessary for an officer to have more than one familiar mount available for service. One of McClellan's favorite "spares" was "Burns", a black stallion named for the friend who gave him to the general. "Burns" had the unusual habit of bolting for home at dinner time, wherever he was, so McClellan had to be careful not to ride him late in the afternoon.

---

around in order to make his force appear stronger, but there was no need to do so. The only firing he encountered was from some skirmishers of a Maryland regiment along Western Run. When he pulled his own men back out of range, the firing ceased.

It was not long before search parties from both sides began to move out cautiously to begin bringing in the wounded. General Early observed that "The parties from both armies gradually approached each other and continued their removal work without molestation from either side, being apparently appalled for a moment into cessation from all hostile purposes by the terrible spectacle presented to view." It was not long before some Confederate officer sent a white flag forward to establish a truce, to which Averell readily agreed. Averell's description of the grisly battlefield that morning is indeed moving: "Our ears had been filled with agonizing cries from thousands before the fog was lifted, but now our eyes saw an appalling spectacle upon the slopes down to the woodlands half a mile away. Over five thousand dead and wounded men were on the ground in every attitude of distress. A third of them were dead or dying, but enough were alive and moving to give to the field a singular crawling effect. The different stages of the ebbing tide are often marked by the lines of flotsam and jetsam left along the seashore. So here could be seen three distinct lines of dead and wounded marking the last front of three Confederate charge of the night before."

The truce actually worked to Averell's advantage as it secured his safety and won more time for the army to withdraw to Harrison's Landing. At about 1000, when he heard that Keyes' corps at the rear of the retiring column was over two miles away, Averell began withdrawing his small command. Lee had issued orders for Jackson and Longstreet to conduct a pursuit, but none could be effectively mounted. Jackson needed all day just to get his command organized enough to begin marching, and by the time Longstreet got his men together the rainstorm had made such a mess of the roads that he was able to advance only two miles. Later in the day Lee wisely called off the pursuit in order to let the men rest.

Apparently the only Confederate officer truly interested in pursuing the retreating Union army was Jeb Stuart. Stuart met Lee on the cold morning of 2 July at the Poindexter House north of Malvern Hill, where the commander had established an indoor headquarters in order to get out of the rain. Stuart had been north of the Chickahominy for three days following the battle of Gaines' Mill on 27 June, and his men had gorged themselves on abandoned Union food and supplies left at McClellan's former base at White House. His presence was sorely needed south of the Chickahominy, but he did not take it on his own initiative to return because he was too busy gathering plunder and trying to locate Union positions north of the river. When Lee finally recalled him late on 30 June, it took him a full day to reach Malvern Hill because of the congested roads in the army's rear. That was unfortunate, for his services could have been used on 1 July when Lee wanted to investigate the possibility of marching east of Malvern Hill instead of confronting the Union army drawn up there.

Stuart's men were exhausted from their long day's march on 1 July, but their commander was ready to throw them at once into action. Stuart received Lee's approval to advance and harass the enemy, and set off at once. He was delighted to capture "scores of the discomfited and demoralized foe at every turn" and even caught one crew member of the *Monitor* who was ashore with his warship in plain view on the river. Stuart advanced until his progress was stopped by two regiments of Sickles' *Excelsior Brigade*. That evening and the next morning he found and verified the location of McClellan's new lines at Harrison's Landing and reported them to Lee. At 0800 on 3 July he startled the soggy Union camps by lobbing a few shells across over their tents from across Herring Creek. He had indeed found a favorable site from which to bombard the Union lines, but he could not hold it in the face of an advancing infantry brigade and fire from the gunboats in the river. At 1400 he had no choice but to withdraw. He withdrew two miles and went into camp.

It was not until the morning of 4 July that Jackson and Longstreet brought their infantry up to face McClellan's lines. By then the Union position was too firmly entrenched to be attacked, and Lee recognized the fact. In the next three days he made arrangements to try to bombard the Union shipping in the James but could accomplish nothing of importance. When McClellan's troops did not stir from their lines, Lee at

View of the Federal encampment at Harrison's Landing.

length withdrew his army to Richmond on 8 July.

Lee had indeed won a great victory by driving McClellan back from Richmond and preventing him from instituting a siege. Nevertheless, he was disappointed that his victory was not more complete. In his campaign report, filed on 6 March 1863, he noted that "Under ordinary circumstances the Federal army should have been destroyed." The principal reasons for this disappointment, he stated, were "the want of correct and timely information" and "the character of the country." Nowhere did he blame the failures of his principal subordinates, almost every one of whom had made at least one major error during the course of the campaign. Instead, he praised God for the results he did achieve, and claimed the capture of 10,000 prisoners, 52 pieces of artillery, upwards of 35,000 stands of small arms, and stores and supplies of every description. McClellan's losses, though, did not exceed Lee's, as the Confederate general believed. The Confederates actually lost 20,141 men (3,286 killed, 15,909 wounded, and 946 missing) during the Seven Days Battles, while Union losses came to 15,849 (1,734 killed, 8,062 wounded, and 6,053 missing).

It took McClellan's troops several days to regain their composure once they reached their soggy camps at Harrison's Landing. Their spirits began to revive when they received fresh rations—many had not eaten since before the battle at Malvern Hill. They were also pleased to see the rains let up at last, and they were especially happy that Lee was no longer attacking and they were no longer retreating. McClellan tried to cheer them up by having all the army's bands play on 4 July, the nation's birthday. One New York soldier noted that "To the soldiers McClellan was less a hero now, perhaps, than before, but he was more a martial leader than ever."

McClellan's army was ready to resume the campaign within a week of Malvern Hill, but their leader was not. McClellan sent letter after letter to Lincoln and Stanton begging for reinforcements, citing Lee's great strength and his own losses, which included 18,000 sick according to his Medical Director, Jonathan Letterman. When his chief of staff, Brigadier General Randolph Marcy, went to Washington and overstated his case by hinting that McClellan might be forced to surrender if he did not receive reinforcements, President Lincoln decided that it was time for him to visit the army and see the situation for himself. He reviewed the *Army of the Potomac* at Harrison's Landing on 8 July and was pleased to see that it was in much better shape than he expected; he was astute enough to discern that the morale of the men was much better than that of their commander. He also realized that McClellan had no detailed plans for continuing the campaign or for cooperating with John Pope's newly created army that had been formed on 26 June to protect Washington.

Before Lincoln returned to Washington, McClellan had the audacity to give him a letter outlining his military and political views on the progress of the war. McClellan was clearly lobbying to get his old job back as general-in-chief, since he

Lincoln reviews the Army of the Potomac *on 8 July. The president found the army in better shape than he expected after the recent defeats.*

was certainly in no position to be dealing out advice after his recent defeats in the field. His effort was totally unsuccessful, as Lincoln appointed Major General Henry Halleck to that position the day after he returned to Washington from Harrison's Landing. Halleck came to visit McClellan on 25 July to discuss strategy and was disappointed to learn that McClellan still had no definite plans. He talked briefly of moving against Petersburg or having Pope's army come down to the Peninsula; what he really wanted was to be reinforced to 300,000 men so that he could move again on Richmond. At length Halleck told McClellan to decide between continuing the campaign with minimal reinforcements or withdrawing to northern Virginia. When McClellan delayed at making his decision, Halleck on 30 July ordered him to begin evacuating his sick. McClellan belatedly began an advance to Malvern Hill on 2 August, but by then it was too late to please Halleck, who on the next day ordered the *Army of the Potomac* to leave Harrison's Landing and march to Fort Monroe for transportation to Alexandria.

McClellan's withdrawal up the Peninsula consumed almost three weeks. The *V Corps* embarked at Fort Monroe on 20 August, followed by the *III Corps* on the 21st, the *VI Corps* on the 23rd and 24th, the *II Corps* on the 26th, and most of the *IV Corps* on the 29th. Only one division of the army, Peck's of the *IV Corps*, was left behind at Yorktown to guard the approaches to Fort Monroe. The Confederates did not harass McClellan's withdrawal, and indeed were glad to see him go. Lee took full advantage of the situation to head north and strike Pope's army in the campaign that would lead to the Confederate triumph at Second Bull Run and an invasion of Maryland.

McClellan's Life After 1860

When the Civil War broke out in late 1860, George B. McClellan was living in Cincinnati and was serving as superintendent of the Ohio and Mississippi Railroad. His organizational skills and varied military experiences caused him to be very much in demand, and he was considered for appointment to high command by the governors of several states including New York, Pennsylvania, Ohio and Illinois. Reportedly he was most interested in becoming the commander of Pennsylvania's state militia. On 23 April 1861 he was on his way to apply for the post, which was his for the asking, when he stopped to see Ohio's governor William Dennison in Columbus. Dennison was quite impressed with his abilities and offered him an appointment as major general in command of Ohio's militia. McClellan was flattered and promptly accepted after the state legislature promptly passed a bill in his favor that very day. One can only wonder how differently the war might have gone had McClellan turned Dennison down and become a general in Pennsylvania instead.

As it turned out, McClellan was a lucky man to be in the right place at the right time. He was an able administrator and soon won an appointment as a brigadier general in the Regular Army. His command was the Department of the Ohio, which also included Kentucky and western Virginia. He organized the campaign that successfully occupied much of western Virginia and claimed credit for the victories his troops won at Rich Mountain (11 July) Carrick's Ford (13 July), though he was not personally present at either battle. The two victories laid the foundation for the creation of a pro-Union government in western Virginia and led directly to the formation of the state of West Virginia in 1863.

McClellan's successful West Virginia campaign won him national attention, and he seemed to be a shining star after McDowell met defeat at First Bull Run on 21 July. McClellan was called to Washington the next day to take command of the army there, and on 1 November succeeded the aged Winfield Scott as general in chief of the Union armies. He did an excellent job at reorganizing McDowell's army and restoring morale, and deserves full credit for establishing the *Army of the Potomac* as a fighting machine that would serve the North so well until the end of the war. It was one thing, though, to create the machine and quite another thing to see it battered in battle. McClellan's greatest weakness would be his reluctance to take aggressive action, whether in front of Washington in late 1861, at Yorktown in April 1862, during the retreat to the James in late June 1862, or at Antietam in September 1862. A significant cause of his reluctance to engage the enemy was his sincere belief that he was always heavily outnumbered by the Confederates (see sidebar "The Numbers Game").

As discussed in the text, McClellan developed a bold strategy to make a seaborne movement to Fort Monroe, but lost all his advantage when he allowed himself to become bogged down at Yorktown. It seems that his textbook training and experiences in Europe led him to believe too much in the value of siege warfare. Indeed, he might have successfully besieged Richmond if any general less aggressive than Lee had been in charge of the Confederate army. Lee appreciated the seriousness of the situation and took advantage of McClellan's awkward dispositions to defeat the right wing of the Union army and drive McClellan's whole force away from Richmond to Harrison's Landing.

As discussed in the text, McClellan was totally outgeneraled by Lee in the Seven Days Battles, but the Federal general was still in a position to renew his movement on Richmond. It is interesting to conjecture what might have happened had he done so, and whether or not he could have been as successful as Grant would be two years later at besieging Richmond and Petersburg. As it was, Lincoln lost confidence in McClellan and Lee exploited the situation to defeat John Pope's Army of Virginia at Second Bull Run on 29-30 August 1862.

Much of the *Army of the Potomac* was in transit back to northern Virginia at the height of the Second Bull Run campaign, and the troops that did reach the battlefield admittedly did not cooperate well with Pope. Pope's defeat left Lincoln with little choice but to keep McClellan in command of an expanded *Army of the Potomac* that absorbed Pope's army. McClellan saw a chance to redeem his reputation and gladly accepted the challenge. He restored the morale of his men and led them into Maryland to face Lee's first invasion of the North. His quarrel with the War Department over the use of the garrison at Harpers Ferry resulted in the loss of 12,000 men and 73 cannons to Jackson's Confederate command. At the height of the campaign McClellan again showed his characteristic reluctance to engage the enemy. He was spurred to action only by the chance discovery of a copy of Lee's campaign orders in a field near Frederick, Maryland. He used the information to win the battle of South Mountain on 14 September, but did not press his advantage the next day. It seems amazing today that he was unable to destroy Lee's much smaller army at Antietam during the war's bloodiest day of fighting on 17 September; he firmly believed that the Confederate army outnumbered his command and refused to take risks or commit to action the reserves that would have carried the day.

When McClellan refused to pursue Lee after Antietam, Lincoln again lost confidence in him and allowed him to remain in command only until he was able to persuade Ambrose Burnside to take charge of the army on 7 November 1862.

"Little Mac" never held field command again. As he and his favorite generals fell into disfavor in late 1862 and early 1863, he turned to politics to satisfy his ambitions. He was a life long Democrat and permitted himself to be nominated as his party's presidential candidate in 1864, even though he did not agree with the Democrats' peace platform. His campaign turned out to be a disaster, as he won 45 percent of the popular vote but carried only three states, Delaware, New Jersey and Kentucky. He also lost the respect of many of the soldiers who had once cherished him; Lincoln carried the soldier vote by a wide plurality.

After the war ended, McClellan led a successful career as a civil engineer. He travelled extensively and was even elected Governor of New Jersey (1878-1881). His greatest concern, however, was to redeem his tarnished reputation. For this purpose he published his memoirs, *McClellan's Own Story*, in 1887, a poorly organized, very biased account that dodged many important issues of his military career. He died in Orange, New Jersey, on 29 October 1885 and is buried in Trenton along with his wife and father-in-law, Randolph B. Marcy (1812-1887), who had served as his chief of staff during the Peninsular campaign.

The Battlefields Today

Some Civil War Battlefield Parks such as Gettysburg, Shiloh and Pea Ridge contain about 4,000 acres, and the biggest, Chickamuaga and Chattanooga National Military Park, has over 8,000 acres. The Richmond National Battlefield Park, created in 1944, contains only 800 acres even though it includes sites from McClellan's 1862 campaign, Grant's 1864-1865 campaign, and various hospitals and forts in Richmond. Only about 200 acres of this total includes ground from the Seven Days Battles. About 60 acres, less than one-tenth of the battlefield, preserves the left portion of the Union line at Gaines' Mill, in the area where Hood's brigade broke Porter's line late on 27 June 1862. About 131 acres of the Malvern Hill battlefield are owned by the park at the center of the battlefield area near the Crew House and the West House. Much of the battlefield land outside the park boundaries remains similar to its wartime appearance, particularly near Malvern Hill and White Oak Swamp, and the various stages and impor-

tant sites of the campaign are well marked by historical markers erected by the state of Virginia. However, there is no guarantee that these battle areas will not be lost in the future. Much of the battlefield of Seven Pines is now a highway interchange, and there is a major housing development near Gaines' Mill located in the Confederate staging area only one-half mile from Boatswain's Creek and the same distance from the 1864 Cold Harbor battlefield.

The origins of the Richmond National Battlefield Park date to 1932 when some public spirited individuals obtained the present park land and donated it to the state of Virginia. Perhaps some historically minded philanthropist or preservation groups will be able to expand the park at a future date in spite of spiraling land costs. If you want to help, contact either The Conservation Fund, Civil War Battlefield Campaign, 1800 North Kent Street, Suite 1120, Arlington, Virginia 22209, or Civil War Round Table Associates, PO Box 7388, Little Rock, Arkansas 72217.

Bibliography

There is unfortunately no single comprehensive, unbiased study of the Peninsula campaign and its battles. Alexander S. Webb's *The Peninsula* (New York, 1881) is short, dated and biased on the Union side. Clifford Dowdey's *The Seven Days: The Emergence of Lee* (New York, 1964) is very readable but does not present the early stages of the campaign or the Union point of view. The only recent survey of the campaign is Joseph R. Cullen's *The Peninsula Campaign, 1862: McClellan and Lee, the Struggle for Richmond* (Harrisburg, 1973), which is too short (well under 200 pages long) to deal in detail with the campaign's numerous battles.

The only monograph available on any of the campaign's battles is *The Battle of Seven Pines* by General G.W. Smith (New York, 1881); this is largely argumentative and quotes heavily from published battle reports. It is frustrating that the campaign has not sparked enough scholarly interest to spawn individual studies of such interesting battles as Yorktown, Williamsburg, Gaines' Mill, Savage Station, Frayser's Farm and Malvern Hill, all of which were as important as more studied battles from later years in the war. Gaines' Mill is particularly in need of a major study since it is difficult to reconstruct the several stages of the battle from primary sources and more recent studies.

Perhaps the fullest account of the campaign is found in Douglas Southall Freeman's ground breaking and well written study, *Lee's Lieutenants: A Study in Command* (New York, 1942). *Volume I: Manassas to Malvern Hill*, provides an important analysis of the key stages of the campaign and the characteristics and abilities of all the Confederate officers down to the brigade level and beyond. Freeman's examination of Jackson's exhaustion and Magruder's health problems are particularly enlightening, and he clearly lays out how poor Confederate staff work helped to frustrate Lee's plans. Freeman's battle accounts are perhaps the most detailed available on the Confederate side, and he does a superior job at showing the difficulties and obstacles that the officers and soldiers faced at the time. We can only regret that there is no comparable study available on the Union army during the campaign.

Biographies of the campaign's leading participants provide informative but by no means comprehensive views of the campaign. The most thorough work on Lee is Douglas Southall Freeman's multi-volume study *R.E. Lee*; the reader, though, should be forewarned that Freeman's interpretations presented in these books do not always agree with those expressed in *Lee's Lieutenants*. More good reading on the great Confederate general is found in *Gray Fox* (New York, 1956) by Burke Davis, and *Lee* (New York, 1965) by Clifford Dowdey. Lee's image as a Confederate hero is thoughtfully if controversially explored by Thomas L. Connelly in *The Marble Man* (New York, 1977). Much fewer studies have been attempted of the North's enigmatic commander during the campaign, *George B. McClellan, Shield of the Union* (Baton Rouge, 1957), by Warren W. Hassler, and *George B. McClellan, The Young Napoleon* (New York, 1988), by Stephen W. Sears.

The following biographies of other leading generals in the campaign will be of interest. On the Confederate side: *A Different Valor, The Story of General Joseph E. Johnston* (New York, 1956) by Govan and Livingood; *Mighty Stonewall* (New York, 1957) by Frank Vandiver; *Lee's Maverick General, Daniel Harvey Hill* (New York, 1961) by Hal Bridges; *General A.P. Hill, The Story of a Confederate Warrior* (New York, 1987) by James Robertson; and *Bold Dragoon, The Life of Jeb Stuart* (New York,

1986), by Emory Thomas. *Jefferson Davis* (New York, 1977) by Clement Eaton also provides good background material for the campaign. Unfortunately, there are few good available biographies of McClellan's leading generals, most of whom fell into disfavor soon after the campaign. Two of his best division commanders were *Kearny the Magnificent* (New York (1962) by Irving Werstein and *Fighting Joe Hooker* (New York, 1941) by Walter H. Hebert.

The best way to study the campaign may well be to read the actual words of the participants themselves. Battle reports for all the officers of both armies from regimental to army level can be found in volume XI of the monumental series *War of the Rebellion: A Compilation of the Official Records of the Union and Confederate Armies* (Washington, 1890-1901). The most interesting of the numerous memoirs written later by the campaign's leading participants is *McClellan's Own Story* (New York, 1886), which is as significant for what it says as for what it does not. Union commander Regis de Trobriand gives a view of the campaign from the battle lines in *Four Years with the Army of the Potomac* (Boston, 1889). Recommended autobiographies by leading Confederate officers in the campaign include: *From Manassas to Appomattox* (Philadelphia, 1896) by James Longstreet; *A Narrative of Military Operations* (New York, 1874) by Joseph E. Johnston, and *Advance and Retreat* (Philadelphia, 1880) by John B. Hood. A number of leading officers on both sides wrote important essays on the campaign for the *Century Magazine* in the 1880s. These were reprinted in volume 2 of *Battles and Leaders of the Civil War* (New York, 1884-1888; reprinted 1956 and later), edited by Johnson and Buel. Notable articles include features by Joe Johnston and G.W. Smith on Seven Pines; Fitz-John Porter and D.H. Hill on Gaines' Mill; William Franklin and James Longstreet on Savage Station and Frayser's Farm; and D.H. Hill on Malvern Hill. Excerpts of personal accounts by soldiers of both sides from privates to generals can be found in the useful volume *Sword Over Richmond, An Eyewitness History of McClel-*

lan's Peninsula Campaign (New York, 1986), by Richard Wheeler.

The following unit histories give lively and detailed accounts of the battles and marches of the campaign. On the Union side: *History of the Pennsylvania Reserve Corps* (Lancaster, 1865) by J.R. Sypher; *Sykes' Regular Infantry Division* (Jefferson, N.C. 1990) by Timothy J. Reese; *History of Kearny's First New Jersey Brigade* (Trenton, 1910) by Camille Baquet; *Vermont in the Civil War* (Burlington, 1886), by G.G. Benedict; and *From Bull Run to Chancellorsville* (New York, 1906) by Newton M. Curtis. The role of the army's artillery in the campaign is discussed in *Grape and Canister* (New York, 1960) by L. Van Loan Naisawald. Sources on the Confederate side include: *History of Kershaw's Brigade* (1899), by Augustus Dickert; *Hood's Texas Brigade* (New York, 1910) by J.B. Polley; *Up Came Hill, The Story of the Light Division and its Leaders* (Harrisburg, 1958), by Martin Schenck; and *History of the Fourth South Carolina Volunteers* (Greenville, 1891), by J.W. Reid. The Role of the Confederate artillery is presented in the *Long Arm of Lee* (Lynchburg, 1915) by Jennings C. Wise. For more on Stuart's ride around McClellan's army, see *The Last Cavaliers* (New York, 1979) by Samuel Carter III.

Order of Battle
with Strength and Casualty Figures

ARMY OF THE POTOMAC
SEVEN DAYS BATTLES

UNIT	STRENGTH	K	W	MC	T
General HQ	1,300	0	0	12	12
Second Corps	17,300	201	1,195	1,024	2,420
(Sumner)					
HQ	100	0	1	0	1
Richardson's Div.	8,100	98	645	541	1,284
Sedgwick's Div.	8,700	103	549	481	1,133
Res. Arty.	400	0	0	2	2
Third Corps	18,900	158	1,021	794	1,973
(Heintzelman)					
HQ and Cav.	800	6	2	3	11
Hooker's Div.	9,400	55	412	263	730
Kearny's Div.	8,300	96	604	527	1,227
Res. Arty.	400	1	3	1	5
Fourth Corps	14,700	70	512	218	800
(Keyes)					
HQ and Cav.	700	0	0	0	0
Couch's Div.	8,300	69	510	97	676
Peck's Div.	5,300	1	2	121	124
Res. Arty.	400	0	0	0	0
Fifth Corps	30,300	995	3,805	2,801	7,601
(Porter)					

UNIT	STRENGTH	K	W	MC	T
HQ and Cav.	700	3	9	4	16
Morell's Div.	12,00	479	1,834	819	3,132
Sykes'Div.	6,000	178	703	363	1,244
McCall's Div.	9,500	318	1,176	1,573	3,067
Arty, Res. and Siege Train	2,100	17	83	42	142
Sixth Corps (Franklin)	19,300	296	1,472	1,110	2,878
HQ and Cav.	800	0	0	3	3
Slocum's Div.	9,200	226	1,081	768	2,075
Smith's Div.	9,300	70	391	339	800
Cavalry Res.	2,100	14	55	85	154
Engineers	1,500	0	2	21	23
ARMY TOTAL	105,400	1,734	8,062	6,053	15,849

ARMY OF NORTHERN VIRGINIA
SEVEN DAYS BATTLES

JACKSON'S COMMAND	28,400	1,198	5,389	113	6,700
Cavalry	400	-	-	-	-
Whiting's Div.	4,400	159	1,025	10	1,194
Hood's Brig.	2,000	92	526	5	623
Law's Brig	2,200	66	482	5	553
HQ and Arty.	200	1	17	-	18
Winder's Div.	7,000	148	631	1	780
Stonewall Brig.	1,400	30	149	-	179
Cunningham's Brig.	1,100	1	15	-	16
Fulkerson's Brig.	1,000	2	15	1	18
Lawton's Brig.	3,500	115	452	-	567
Ewell's Div.	6,800	182	753	52	987
Elzey's Brig.	2,000	52	229	3	284
Trimble's Brig.	2,400	71	280	49	400
Taylor's Brig.	2,000	56	236	-	292
Maryland Line	400	3	8	-	11
D.H. Hill's Div.	9,800	709	2,980	50	3,689

UNIT	STRENGTH	K	W	MC	T
Rodes' Brig.	1,600	112	458	-	470
G.B. Anderson's Brig.	1,600	159	704	-	863
Garland's Brig.	1,800	192	637	15	844
Colquitt's Brig.	1,800	75	474	5	544
Ripley's Brig.	2,300	171	707	30	908
Arty.	700	-	-	-	-
MAGRUDER'S COMMAND	13,700	369	1,969	155	2,493
Jones' Div.	4,100	111	718	52	881
Toombs' Brig.	1,600	44	380	6	430
G.T. Anderson's Brig	2,100	64	327	46	437
Arty.	400	3	11	-	14
McLaws' Div.	4,200	101	470	101	672
Semmes' Brig.	2,500	31	121	63	215
Kershaw's Brig.	1,700	70	349	38	457
Magruder's Div.	5,000	157	781	2	940
Cobb's Brig.	3,000	66	347	2	415
Griffith's Brig.	2,000	91	434	-	525
S.D. Lee's Arty.	400	-	-	-	-
LONGSTREET'S DIV.	9,600	766	3,436	237	4,439
Kemper's Brig.	1,400	44	205	165	414
R.H. Anderson's Brig.	1,300	136	638	13	787
Pickett's Brig.	1,500	72	563	19	654
Wilcox's Brig.	1,900	229	806	20	1,055
Pryor's Brig.	1,400	170	681	11	862
Featherston's Brig.	1,300	115	543	9	667
Arty.	800	-	-	-	-
A.P. HILL'S DIV.	14,800	631	3,510	36	4,177
Field's Brig.	1,500	78	500	2	580
Gregg's Brig.	2,500	152	773	4	929
J.R. Anderson's Brig.	2,000	62	300	2	364
Branch's Brig.	3,500	105	706	28	839
Archer's Brig.	2,000	92	443	-	535
Pender's Brig.	2,500	130	692	-	822
Arty.	800	12	96	-	108
HUGER'S DIV.	9,000	305	1,491	359	2,155
Mahone's Brig.	2,700	66	274	124	464

UNIT	STRENGTH	K	W	MC	T
Wright's Brig.	2,200	93	483	90	666
Armistead's Brig.	1,600	51	281	69	401
Ransom's Brig.	2,500	95	453	76	624
HOLMES' DIV.	6,700	2	51	-	53
Daniel's Brig.	1,700	2	22	-	24
Walker's Brig.	3,600	-	12	-	12
Wise's Command	1,000	-	-	-	-
Arty.	400	-	17	-	17
PENDLETON'S ARTY.	2,700	10	35	-	45
Brown's Arty.	600	5	24	-	29
Cutts' Arty.	600	3	6	-	9
Richardson's Arty.	400	1	4	-	5
Nelson's Arty.	400	1	1	-	2
Misc. Arty.	700	-	-	-	-
STUART'S CAV.	3,600	5	26	40	71
ARMY TOTAL	88,500	3,286	15,907	940	20,133

NOTE: This is the first attempt the author is aware of to break down the Confederate army strength at brigade level. All previous estimates have placed the Confederate strength at between 80,000 and 90,000: Freeman gives 85,500; Walter Taylor gives 80,762; E.P. Alexander gives 83,500; Henderson gives 86,500; and D.H. Hill, Jr., gives 86,152. No Confederate muster was taken on 30 June 1862 because of the ongoing campaign, so exact figures are not available. Some casualty figures are incomplete, particularly in the number of missing.

ABBREVIATIONS

Arty.	Artillery
Brig.	Brigade
Cav.	Cavalry
Div.	Division
HQ	Headquarters
K	Killed
MC	Missing or captured
W	Wounded
T	Total

Index